All the Trials of Life

The weird and wonderful journey
of a dynamic healer

by

Jane Tinworth

Photograph by Roger Eaton

Also by Jane Tinworth
The Bridge of Awareness
A compilation of the Teachings of Zed

Published in England by World Awareness Trust
2013
www.worldawarenesstrust.org

ISBN 978-0-9568619-1-7

Printed by
Short Run Press Limited
Exeter
www.shortrunpress.co.uk

Foreword

As I began reading Jane Tinworth's autobiographical book All The Trials of Life *increasingly I felt uncomfortable, so revealing are the words in describing many details of her private life. But as I read on it became clear that this frank and open account was about the unfolding of Jane's spiritual awareness and was entirely appropriate in order to provide a foundation of understanding about aspects of her spiritual journey which culminated in the compilation of her beautiful book* The Bridge of Awareness.

Both of Jane Tinworth's books, All the Trials of life and The Bridge of Awareness, are seen as companion books fitting perfectly together, the human link with the spiritual. They are essential reading for those seeking simple, easily understood explanations and guidance about the spiritual nature of life, about subtle energy, the power of thought, and so much more.

It felt as though the secrets of the Universe were being shared with me for my personal benefit that I might more easily grow in spiritual awareness and have greater access to the wisdom which lies within all of us.

Both Zed's words in The Bridge of Awareness *and those of Jane Tinworth in* All the Trials of Life *are very easy to read and understand, written with great compassion, as if speaking gently and directly to the reader with love.*

Brian Weld
Edinburgh

Preface

I had finished compiling The Bridge of Awareness when I was told 'break down the barriers you have to writing about yourself.' I was aware that readers of the 'Bridge' would naturally be curious about the origin of the spiritual philosophy it contains but the thought of actually exposing my personal involvement to public gaze was not something I relished. On the other hand I know that spirit asks nothing of me without good reason. I therefore set myself to the task, and with surprising results, for as I wrote I was able to see a broader picture for myself and particularly how the unusual dynamic response to my healing has played an important part in the overall plan.

There has also been an additional benefit for me, best described in this passage from Levi Dowling's book, The Aquarian Gospel of Jesus the Christ, where the master Elihu is speaking to his pupils:

'If you would ask me what to study I would say, yourselves; and when you had well studied them, and then would ask me what to study next, I would reply, yourselves.'

My hope is that this story of my journey, thus far, will provide food for thought on your journey too.

Some of the names have been changed where appropriate, but none of the facts.

Jane Tinworth.
2012

'All the trials of life are meaningless unless you learn from them'

'Zed'

Chapter 1

My sense of wonder at the power of dynamic healing has never left me. However, in the beginning I was quite unprepared for what was to happen when I received a call one Saturday morning in September 1987 from a local hotelier, asking if I would see one of his guests who had arrived from Wales with a 'bad back'. I can't recall how this hotelier knew I was a healer, perhaps I had previously treated someone in his family, but clearly he was sufficiently moved by this man's plight to suggest I might be able to help. We arranged that he would bring his guest over that morning and as soon as they appeared around the corner of the house I could see this was no temporary affliction but one of long-standing.

Bill Hoskins was a tall, lean man well into his sixties whose posture and lined and sallow complexion spoke of chronic suffering. With the aid of his walking stick and the doorframe he managed to mount the one step into the house and walk slowly and painfully across the hallway to a chair in my healing room. He also had difficulty in breathing and so it was a little while before he recovered sufficiently to tell me his story.

Bill told me that he had gone down the pit as a teenage lad and worked hard at the coalface for 30 years, often knee-deep in water and inhaling dust until eventually his lungs gave out with the miners scourge of pnuemoniconiosis and he was forced to go 'on the sick'. Faced with what he considered idleness, he searched for suitable employment and eventually secured a position of responsibility at an engineering works where he was very happy. Then came the day when a steel gantry ladder was dislodged and came crashing down, striking him on the head and sending him reeling across the factory floor and into the wall 'like a skittle' he said. His injuries meant the end of his treasured occupation and the start of twelve long years of pain and frustration despite the best efforts of the medical profession. Apart from the problem with his lungs, Bill now suffered memory loss, periodic shaking of his right arm, agonising pain in his lower back that sometimes put him in bed for several days, and such severe pain in his right hip and leg that both standing and walking were difficult. This was obvious that day as he moved carefully from the chair to lie down on my treatment couch.

Bill had no experience of healing and so I took time to explain that my function was simply to create a kind of space, or environment, that would help his body to heal itself in whatever way and to whatever degree was possible or appropriate. I told him that whatever happened would happen naturally and without direction from my mind or his. I asked him to close his eyes and to relax as much as he could and I began to move my hands a little distance above his body, never touching but just silently sensing the constantly changing reactions in his energy field. Immediately he felt warmth on his head and neck and a feeling of deep relaxation spreading throughout his body. Then over the next 50 minutes the gentle sensations of heat and tingling changed to phases of quite extreme heat or cold or pain and then very powerful physical movements of a kind I had never before witnessed and which took me completely by surprise.

Very soon I took a step back and simply observed what was happening. At one point Bill began to shake so violently with his head banging up and down on the couch that I thought he was having some kind of fit and, feeling concerned, I bent down and quietly asked him if this had happened to him before. Through clenched teeth he replied that it had not and he told me, "I am in your hands, I am content." Those words moved me deeply and I resolved that if he could put so much trust in me, then I would trust in the healing power working through me.

There are no words to adequately describe an experience where on one hand there is complete mental and physical relaxation while on the other hand the body is performing spontaneous movements and contortions, some of which would tax the abilities of a trained athlete, let alone someone weak and in poor health. I remember at one stage watching in awe as Bill's body undulated rapidly from head to foot as if two people were shaking out a blanket. Finally his right leg began to rotate at about 45 degrees from his body before pulling quite violently from the hip outwards and drawing the knee right up so he was forced to lie on his left side. I was then aware of a feeling of great peace and knew the session was finished.

The atmosphere in the room was absolutely still. After a while Bill pushed himself up and swivelled round to sit on the end of the couch. "I feel different, I feel so different" he said quietly. There really wasn't much else to say. He slid gently to his feet and walked around the room before going to stand by the window and stare through the glass at nothing. I knew he was crying and tears welled up in my eyes too. "I never thought I would feel like this again" he said. The feeling in the room was indescribable.

A few minutes later Bill walked upright from the room, strode across the hallway and handed his walking stick to his friend. "I shan't be needing this again" he told him.

I later referred to this event as my first full-blown session of *dynamic healing* – a term that seemed to fit this physically active response to the healing. I spent the next two days completely and utterly exhausted.

Three days later Bill returned for a second session, after which we recorded his enthusiastic response, spoken in his strong Welsh accent. This is the transcript of the recording: my questions are shown in brackets.

[Tell me how you've been since I saw you?] "Fantastic! I can't believe it. The wife can't believe it. Only yesterday we walked from the ferry into the town and at dinner the wife told the lady at the digs, 'I can't believe it, I haven't seen the boy walk like that for 14 years', which is true. I've had nothing – just one or two little clicks, which you said we would have, which I don't know whether it's bones going back in but it's a fantastic feeling and I laugh inside. I've had one or two little aches but perhaps I did walk a bit too far – well, I did – but I feel elated, there's no other word for it because I've been in pain for 14 years ever since my accident. I've tried to fathom it out but we know it's you, we know what you've done for me and the wife knows and all the people in the digs, because when I was down there I was a cripple and I couldn't get off the chair or the settee unless I rolled onto the floor and got up like a child. Fabulous – out of this world!

[How have you managed over the past years?] Well, with the accident, the bottom discs in base of the spine are gone and when I went up to see the specialist he said with an operation I could be in a damn sight more pain after so I didn't want no-one to touch it. About 5 or 6 weeks ago I had a terrible attack and I couldn't move. The wife was sat on the settee and she would have to get off so I could lie on the settee then roll off onto the floor and get up like a little child and I was in agony. I didn't think I'd be able to come on holiday but thank the Lord He allowed me to come otherwise I wouldn't have met you and got out of this pain. What I've suffered in the last 14 years – they can give you tablets and things but it's nothing like I've had here.

[What about the shaking you've had?] I haven't had the shakes – there you are – my hands are steady as a rock. And (before) my wife has had to put my food back in the oven because I couldn't pick my knife and fork up with the shakes.

[How is your breathing?] Not too bad but I'm still puffing going up hills, but that's pnuemoniconiosis and I don't think that will ever alter. But now I can get about, which I couldn't before. And I haven't used my stick: I've got no intention of using it, I've got no inclination of picking it up anyway because I don't want one. It's fantastic – no other word for it. The wife is over the moon, we've phoned London and told the sister-in-law and they can't believe it. The daughter and her husband, they've gone out to Israel on holiday and she wants to see her father without the stick so I don't know what the grandchildren are going to say when I go home. I feel I don't want the stick again – I'm going to put the two of them on the wall.

[Have you found difficulty playing with your grandchildren?] No, I've always been active. But you can only go so far with them, like D....., he's 13 now but when he was 18 months/2 year old, just before I had my accident, we always had a real bit of fun – all the family, the son, the daughter and their children. I have had a bit of difficulty but I take them fishing, so I haven't got to put a lot of energy into that. Now I can go home and we can chase trout – and salmon!

[Do you feel brighter in yourself now?] Well, Gordon, the man that brought me here, said 'Look at Bill's face – it's beaming!' Well, it *was* beaming and it's still beaming and I'm still on cloud nine – that's the only answer. And I'm afraid I'm going to get hurt – but I know I'm not going to get hurt, but I haven't got no worries – I don't want to go back to that old stick or anything like that. I'll take your telephone number and if ever I feel in that condition again I'll have to jump on the first train.

[Hopefully that will never happen.] Thank the Lord, thank the Lord."

Bill came to see me again before he left for home. I asked him how he'd been and again recorded his response:

"Since I came last time I'm remembering my words better, which before I couldn't put a sentence together properly. It seems to be dropping back into place. And the beauty of it is, I'm enjoying it! It's fabulous! I know I'm better now – it's the finest thing that's ever happened to me since the day I was born.

[You've just had another session: that was pretty violent in places, wasn't it?] Oh yes, I could feel my head going all different ways and in the middle of it, it's something you can't explain to anybody – they've got to have that feeling themselves, this traumatic experience due to the fact that every part of your body is moving – it's like a jigsaw puzzle being reassembled – and this is what has happened to me. I must have been in a diabolical state when I first came here – well I knew the pain I was in. Well, thank the Lord that pain has gone.

[Did it hurt while you were going through that 'convulsion' just now?] No, no, no: it was an experience, but no pain. Your body was telling you something, that it was doing something, in your mind all the time telling you that something was wrong, wasn't in place.

[At one stage you said you felt as though you'd been somewhere else while that was happening.] I did, because I can remember getting on the couch and I can remember you starting and that gentle feeling that I had, going into like a coma but still with all your faculties upstairs, but you were going somewhere else, you were riding. And conscious all the time but being somewhere else – it's definitely I've been somewhere else other than on that couch there. A wonderful, wonderful experience. Nothing bad about it at all: the two sessions – fantastic!

[So you wouldn't be afraid to have healing again?] Oh no! If only other people had the faith in it! There hasn't been a bigger blasphemer than me. Well, you can imagine, working down the pit as a boy of 13 back in the '30's and the traumatic experience in '26 when our fathers couldn't go down the pit and we were nigh starving. But ah, that was a wonderful feeling and anybody that don't try it, they're fools, they are actual fools, because there *is* healing, and it's gentle, and it works."

The effects of the healing were maintained and Bill remained well and active until he contracted lung cancer and eventually died a few years later. He had not jumped onto the first train at that diagnosis but had waited until further medical treatment would be useless before contacting me. The healing was as strong as ever and his chest swelled out as his damaged lungs appeared to fill with air but he kept repeating 'I feel so bitter, I feel so bitter' and he returned home to die. However, his wife Jenny later wrote to tell me that the intervening months since our first meeting had been some of the happiest they had spent together.

Would the outcome have been different if Bill had jumped onto the first train? I very much doubt it, for although the motivation for healing is obviously to alleviate suffering, its spiritual objective is even deeper and does not override an individual's determined pathway in life, including the time of their departure. However, it would be several years and in different circumstances that I would come to better understand that fundamental question asked by all humankind: if an all-powerful God of Love exists then why does He allow us to suffer?

Bill Hoskins and Jenny after his second healing session.

Chapter 2

Like most of the really important events in our lives, the realisation of my healing ability came as a complete surprise. The idea of being a healer was not some desire or fancy on my part but an indisputable fact that shot up to the surface like a cork and simply refused to go down again. This is not to say that I was averse to the notion and it certainly didn't seem wrong, it was just that such a prospect was beyond my imagination and therefore brought a confusion of feelings that ranged from elation to doubt. The healers I knew about were famous. I had read everything I could about them: their huge public demonstrations, the miracles they performed on the sick and disabled, their powers of psychic perception and partnerships with spirit helpers. Could I really aspire to be part of this amazing world?

In the Great Britain of the mid 20th century, such activities as mediumship and healing other than the laying on of hands in a church were scorned by the majority of people and actively denounced by the medical establishment and Orthodox religion. Fortunately, this failed to deter a significant minority of the population who sought relief from their pain, grief and unawareness through less conventional avenues. Foremost amongst these alternatives was the Christian Spiritualist Movement, which kept alive the integrity of spiritual healing when it might otherwise have withered quietly away, although their main thrust was then, as now, the evidence that life continues after physical death.

I had, in any case, been drawn to what might be loosely termed the 'unexplained' since childhood and can recall standing in our kitchen at the age of about eight thinking 'I don't belong here' but not even understanding what the thought meant or where it was I was supposed to belong. It seemed such a small and petty thing to stick so firmly in my mind for so many years until I came across Wordsworth's ode 'Intimations of Immortality from Recollections of Early Childhood'. Here I seemed to recognise a familiarity with the words, 'Our birth is but a sleep and a forgetting: The Soul that rises with us, our life's star, hath had elsewhere its setting, and cometh from afar.' Wordsworth goes on to write of shades of the prison house beginning to close upon the growing boy, and of course that is exactly what happens as we move into earthly life with all its challenges and delights, and we turn our backs on our inner reality. It is the journey of physical experience and yet that illusive memory of spirit may remain, albeit stronger for some than for others.

The issue of food also played a major role in my childhood because it reinforced my sense of being somehow different. I refused to eat meat; an instinctive vegetarian in a society where steak and kidney pudding and the Sunday roast were top of the culinary list. Vegetarian recipes were unheard of in our family and it was therefore a case of either eating what was on the table or going without; it was as simple as that. My mother and other well-meaning adults would occasionally try me with meat or other dislikes but my teeth were kept firmly clenched and on the whole I lived on potatoes and cheese and little else. I can remember feeling hungry and weak as a little girl, even though I was rather spherical in shape. The half-mile walk to and from school every day from the age of five or six stays in my mind as a terribly tiring trudge, which is now understandable because I must have been lacking the healthy nourishment necessary to a growing child. I was quite often ill.

My family was no stranger to what might be called non-physical experiences though. My three older sisters, Pamela, Lois and Shirley, all displayed varying degrees of psychic or healing abilities during their lifetimes, leading me in later in life to look further into such genetic links. I came to believe that my maternal grandmother, who died long before I was born, was also a healer in her own way and my mother used to recount how in spite of their own straightened circumstances in the tenements of London during the First World War, her mother was the kind of person that others turned to for help. She recalled the time when they went to visit a sick person where bugs could be seen crawling up the walls of the room and her mother whispered to her, 'Pretend you don't notice'. However, it was my sister Shirley, four years my senior, who became aware of her psychic perceptions at an early age, although it was never something we shared as children. Indeed, it was only in our adult years that she told me about an early experience that she and her best friend had with 'the ghost boy'. My sister has acute memory recall and this is a summary of her account:

'Jean and I had been friends since junior school and played together practically every day. We spent many happy times in the park, a safe place to be in those days. Sometimes we would come across friends to play with. It's amazing to think that sixty years ago there didn't seem to be many people about. We liked to play on the allotments, crawling on our stomachs along the narrow turf paths where we could not be seen, and only occasionally stealing a carrot. One day, after playing in the area (the American Gardens) we walked along the path edged with large bushes and came out at Valentines Mansion where there was a fairly small circular lawn covered with daisies. There was no one else about so we sat down and made daisy chains. We soon got tired of this and just as we were leaving we saw a young boy standing quite still, next to the house.

'The boy was shorter than us but about the same age I would guess, about ten (this was probably 1945). He was very clean and tidy with short dark hair, tight black jacket, large white collar, long tight trousers that stopped above his ankles and black pump type shoes. He looked quite forlorn. Somehow we just accepted him and one of us asked him if he'd like to play. He didn't answer but just looked up to his right. We followed his eyes and saw a thin man, who seemed tall to us, at the top of what appeared to be a metal staircase. The man was standing there, holding on with his right hand, dressed in black with the jacket buttoned high but still showing a little white; his hair was dark. He just nodded but didn't speak and neither did the boy, so we just said 'come on' or something similar and walked off towards the allotments with the boy a couple of steps behind. We weren't fazed about them or their appearance, although looking back now I suppose it was rather strange.

'Jean and I talked together and included the boy but I can't remember him saying anything. I'm sure he didn't. I think we crossed a wide path and were in the open, heading for the allotments, when we turned to talk to the boy again, but he had gone. We looked around and there was no one there at all. We walked back to a large tree to see if he was hiding but he had simply disappeared. We must have taken this is our stride because it didn't scare us and we always referred to him afterwards as the 'Ghost Boy'. It was not a frightening experience.'

I think that one of the most interesting aspects of this event is that both girls had the same experience but Shirley said that she and her friend Jean were always on the same wavelength. Another interesting point is that in latter times Valentines Mansion was the focus of much paranormal investigation before being re-occupied and renovated to its former Georgian elegance. An external metal fire escape was removed by Redbridge Council in 2000.

The park in which the Mansion stood was at the end of our road and played an important part in our young lives in giving us the freedom to run and play in spite of the 'Keep Off the Grass' notices. It also had an open-air swimming pool, a proper bandstand and an enclosure with a stage for visiting song and dance troupes and magicians. There was also a boating lake where young people tended to congregate and where Shirley spent a good deal of time in her teens skilfully skimming across the water in the streamlined skiffs. It was here she met a young man named Tony who had similar psychic talents to herself and this led to regular meetings with him and his mother who was of like persuasion. Some years later I went on a date with Tony, by then an officer in the merchant navy, and was invited to Sunday tea at their flat. After we had eaten and cleared the table, Tony's mother said, 'Shall we sit?' which I thought was a strange thing to say because we were already sitting; they in armchairs on either side the fireplace and me in the middle. What followed made an enormous impression on this teenage girl and helped prepare the way for events that were to unfold.

Tony's mother explained that 'sitting' meant us all relaxing silently and 'attuning to spirit'. I was told that Tony might then appear to drop off to sleep but he would actually be in a trance so that spirit people could come and speak through him and whilst this was happening we must keep calm and answer if spoken to. This sounded peculiar but definitely exciting.

With my chair close to Tony's, I then watched in silent amazement as after just a short time he seemed to fall asleep and the features of this fresh-faced young man began to change and physically re-form until I was sitting next to a lean, aged and weather-beaten Native American Indian. To say that this kind of transfiguration mediumship has to be seen to be believed is obvious but true. Nothing can prepare you for it and suggestions of hypnosis or self-delusion are insulting. The simple truth is that they happen as and when they happen and whether we understand them or not. After all, a mystery is just something for which man has not yet discovered an explanation.

After a little chat with Tony's mother, who addressed him by name and clearly knew him well, the Native Indian turned and asked me to hold out my hand. Reaching out to touch my fingers he said, 'You have great power – use it wisely.' I can't recall what else he said but the sense of gentleness and wisdom in that space was truly wonderful and different from anything I had ever experienced.

After a while of sitting quietly, Tony's features changed again as the Native Indian withdrew, to be moulded this time into the broad face of a Maori, who Tony's mother again addressed by name. Obviously another regular visitor. Suddenly the Maori made a loud guttural noise and leapt out of the chair and into a powerful pose with knees bent and legs and arms akimbo, quickly followed by Tony's mother who sprang into position on the hearthrug with arms outstretched in front of the mantelshelf. 'Quick,' she told me, 'come and put your arms out like this – he sometimes knocks the ornaments off.' And there then followed a quite hilarious episode with this entity grunting, grimacing and performing a rigorous dance around the room whilst Tony's mother and I tried to protect the china knick-knacks from his energetic movements. This was in the days before the All Blacks rugby team performed their famous pre-match Haka on television and so it wasn't until I happened to see an old black and white movie about New Zealand that I recognised the origins of the dance I had witnessed all those years before in a small upstairs flat.

My romance with Tony was short-lived but the effect of his mediumship was lasting and stood me in good stead.

Teenage years tend to be a mixture of over-confidence and anxiety as we navigate our emotions through the rough straights between childhood and adulthood. Mine were no different. For years my best friend was my cousin Anthony, a few months my senior, who lived in a house just across the park with his sisters and brother. Now in our young adulthood we listened to jazz together, jived in dance halls and drove a variety of cars, most of which would now grace a museum. We also tried to discuss the deeper issues of life without actually knowing where to start or what we were looking for, except that we hadn't found it at Sunday school or church, both of which we had attended regularly. On one of our forays into understanding the mind, we asked at the local library for books on telepathy, only to be told rather stiffly that books like *that* were kept in the basement and would have to be signed for.

I was by now working for a large company in the centre of London and just before my 18th birthday I was transferred to a different office to work for a boss who also became a good friend. In due course our conversations ranged across spirituality and fringe subjects, one of which is worth recording here. Victor and I decided to try an experiment in telepathy and agreed that at precisely 10 p.m. that evening we would attune to each other from our respective homes in different counties and I would try to impress a picture on his mind that he would then draw and bring in for comparison. Back in the office the following morning Victor had no drawing but an interesting story to report. He admitted that he had completely forgotten our experiment and that he and his wife had decided to have an early night and were asleep by ten o'clock. For no obvious reason, he said, he woke up to see a ball of mist hanging in the air at the foot of the bed. Slowly the mist grew and reformed until first my face and then the top half of my body were clearly visible. This apparition remained for a while before finally dissolving but strangely, this did not appear to phase Victor at all because he said he simply went back to sleep. On my side of the experiment, I had concentrated very, very hard at the appointed time on transmitting a picture of a bright red pillar-box. This image was obviously not received but interestingly, I was able to describe to Victor a peculiar little fireplace set across the corner of the room on the left side of the bed – an unusual feature that existed in reality but of which I could have absolutely no knowledge under ordinary circumstances. Still, we had to admit that our attempt at telepathy was a complete failure. I should perhaps add that although I had an impression of the fireplace, I had none of my boss and his wife in their bed!

My social life when I was not with my cousin or going out with a particular boyfriend revolved around the local Methodist Church with its after-service discussion groups and youth clubs where we met like-minded people, organised outings and staged wonderful variety shows in which I was usually given good singing parts. Being a member of this diverse and supportive congregation was an important part of my life. It was also here that I met my future husband although he had already signed up for a 2-year expedition to the Antarctic, thus providing a not-unwelcome extension of my spinsterhood. In the meantime, my father was at last made a director of the small company for which he had loyally worked for 30 years, prior to it being sold to a larger concern. The proceeds of this sale enabled my parents to finally move from the small rented flat I had grown up in and buy their first house.

Everyone who speaks of my father does so with good humour and warmth, for that is how he made people feel. He adored his wife throughout their long married life and he loved his four daughters with an almost unreasonable pride and provided us with the kind of supportive parenting that my mother lacked due to her own sad and traumatic childhood. My mother used to recount the story of my entry into this life with typical candour. It seems that I was 3propelled to the foot of the bed whilst my father was dragging a reluctant midwife up the street. My mother asked my paternal grandmother, 'What is it?' She had a look and reported, 'A girl.' 'Oh, leave it where it is.' said my mother. And thus I became the disappointing fourth daughter of a woman whose ardent desire from an early age was to have a son.

I cannot say in all honesty that I was eager to be married but it was the norm in the 1960's and so at the age of 23 I followed my sisters into the state of matrimony and eventual motherhood. The birth of our first son Michael was prolonged and difficult and I was grateful for my mother's help when we left hospital. She adored this new grandson and so it was particularly hard for her when we took him before his first birthday to make a new start several hundreds of miles away. A baby brother was born two years later but unfortunately financial insecurity and lack of emotional support left me ill and low in spirits.

By the spring of 1971, my 32nd year, we came to rest in a rented cottage out in the countryside, which was a splendid adventure for our two little boys who were taken to school by bus each weekday and let loose around the adjoining farm and fields in between. Having possession of the only car, my husband was able to devote himself to a challenging new enterprise but for me, poor and away from my family and friends, the isolation was hard. Into this setting the fortnightly arrival of the mobile library service brought an excitement totally disproportionate to its cargo.

The driver of this splendid old vehicle was a kindly man in his 60's, a member of the Spiritualist Movement, who would bring me interesting books along with an intriguing store of anecdotes on his various psychic experiences. My friend provided me with reading on healing and healers such as Harry Edwards, Ted Fricker, George Chapman and the more sensational and questionable 'Arigo – Surgeon with a Rusty Knife'. He also found books on mediums and channelled teachings and various philosophies including those of some of the North American Indian tribes, which appealed greatly to me. I learned how 'absent' healing could be transmitted from healer to patient over any distance with often surprisingly beneficial results. This prompted me to write to Harry Edwards at his Burrows Lea Sanctuary in Surrey on behalf of friends but strangely not for myself, even though I was by then chronically ill with a debilitating duodenal ulcer. But willing though he was, the librarian driver was limited to the books available and these were relatively few. Indeed, I remember wading through old copies of 'The Proceedings of the Society of Psychical Research' for the want of anything more stimulating. Apart from such Papers, it is true to say that most published literature of this genre leaned towards sensational accounts concerning the 3big names of the day who were able to attract huge crowds with their demonstrations of what was commonly known as 'faith healing', many in the audience no doubt attending in the hope of that throw-away-your-crutches miracle cure.

By way of contrast one day, I took out a book on the practice of meditation, a subject on which I was almost totally ignorant. I seem to recall that the book had a different 'feel' to the others and I read it more carefully. Sitting by the fireside in our little cottage one afternoon I decided to try it out and so after checking that I had enough time before the boys returned from school, I followed the instructions and relaxed, breathed deeply and focussed on the image of a lighted candle in front of my closed eyes. Almost immediately I felt the urge to stand up and do something else, feeling disappointed that this meditation stuff hadn't worked. Imagine my shock when I glanced at the clock and discovered that exactly one hour had gone by - had just disappeared without my knowing it. I went around the cottage checking other clocks but there was no mistake – it was an hour since I'd sat down. I'd had my first real experience of meditation, an experience of truly going out of my mind.

However, my reading matter coupled with past experiences around Shirley and Tony had led me to believe that psychic perception was an integral part of what I was seeking, even if I hadn't yet defined it, and being able to communicate with spirit entities or to see and hear what ordinary people like myself could not, seemed very important. I read that George Chapman himself was not a healer but a full-trance medium through whom the deceased Doctor Lang worked. Chapman was actually a Liverpudlian fireman who initially knew nothing of the doctor or of medical practice and yet subsequent research showed that Dr William Lang had been a respected ophthalmic surgeon at the Middlesex Hospital in London between 1880 and 1914 and that Lang's own daughter and granddaughter were able to discuss family details with him (through Chapman) and attest to his identity and mannerisms. The same was true for an elderly patient whom Lang had treated as a child and who was warmly greeted by her childhood name when she arrived for an appointment with Chapman. The often-amazing results of this remarkable healing partnership are well recorded. Treatment was not confined to ophthalmic conditions but included all kinds of ailments, some of which were dealt with through invisible operations performed slightly above the physical body, in what is called the etheric level. The narrative that particularly stuck in my mind was how visitors to Chapman's home would be greeted by a man who would stride across the room to greet them, hold their spectacles up to the light, peer through the lenses and accurately 'read' the prescription – all with his eyes closed.

Perhaps the most famous healer of the day though was Harry Edwards, who unexpectedly discovered his ability for spiritual healing whilst serving in Iraq during the First World War. His down-to-earth, open approach to healing may not have convinced the Archbishops Commission in 1953 but it certainly raised the profile of spiritual healing the world over. As was often the case, the judgements put upon him by church and medicine were shabby, if not downright dishonest at times, but these seemed in no way to affect his public image and eventually he needed a large team of healers and typists to deal with up to 10,000 requests for absent healing every week. Much later in my journey I would come to appreciate how this works and the pressure it can create.

Some time after my meditation experience it occurred to me to ask Harry Edwards for healing for myself. Whether he dealt personally with my letter is unknown but I am certain that the fact that I finally *asked* is as important as the healing that was sent. As Goethe put it, '...the moment one definitely commits oneself then Providence moves too. All sorts of things occur to help one that would otherwise never have occurred. A whole stream of events issues from the decision, raising in one's favour all manner of unforeseen incidents and meetings and material assistance, which no man could have dreamed would have come his way...' Or to put it into other terms, it is necessary to cease prevaricating and tap into the Source.

The stone walls of our cottage were almost a metre thick and with small windows, with the result that the interior was dim and reliant on a small wood burner for warmth for much of the year. As I sat reading by the fire one April afternoon, I was suddenly enveloped by the most beautiful, indescribable feeling of peace and love. I felt someone gently place his hand under my chin and lift my face, and although I could not see him with my eyes, I know I smiled as I looked up at him. At that moment I knew I was completely and utterly *loved* – I was loved and accepted and *known* with a love beyond words. The experience probably lasted for only a few moments but when it ended and I came back from that space I also *knew* from somewhere deep inside that I was a healer. I was also cured of my illness.

It is important to emphasise that this knowing was not the consequence of any reasoning or desire, but the revealing of something that already existed, an indisputable fact that my mind had not been aware of up to that moment. It was like being given a most precious and unexpected gift that you are not sure you deserve.

Over the next few weeks I began to receive comments on my appearance: I looked different. Had I changed my make-up? Coloured my hair? No. I was simply feeling well again and it was like being released from a long dark prison sentence.

The quest for an understanding of spiritual healing now took centre stage in my mind, where it has more or less remained to the present day. At the time I quite naturally attributed my amazing experience and recovery solely to Harry Edwards and his helpers and it would take around twenty more years for a broader understanding to dawn. Meanwhile though, this new and strange awareness that I was a healer rose up from somewhere deep within me but I had no idea what to do next. I had read the books and thought I knew the basics: what I needed was some practice.

These thoughts were churning over in my mind one day as I sat in that same chair by the fireside with one of my three cats sprawled happily across my lap. This particular feline had come from the adjoining farm and various unpleasant symptoms led me to suspect that it had a tapeworm infestation. I thought 'I'll try giving it healing' and without changing position or the rhythm of the stroking I simply 'thought' healing through my hands and into the cat. Within seconds the cat woke up with a yell, leaped off my lap and rushed across the room and onto a windowsill to be let out. I was close on its heels but before I could open the window the cat had been violently and productively sick. That was the end of the tapeworms and the beginning of my healing practice.

With the benefit of hindsight I can see how perfect that first experience of giving healing was because the cat had no expectations, no faith and no thought processes to conjure a placebo effect. My own expectations were low because my mind was filled with doubt and yet here was an instant and lasting result. In fact, if someone had thought long and hard for a way to give me encouragement, that was it.

Chapter 3

My next move was to take myself off to the nearest Spiritualist Church where I knew healing sessions were offered. My first visit coincided with an afternoon service of mediumship and I slid quietly with my shopping bags into a seat at the back of the Church behind two ladies in overcoats and hats. After a short address and a hymn the platform medium began her session of clairaudience ('clear hearing') and like everyone else, I suspect, I desperately hoped there would be a message from the spirit world for me. Words of hope and reassurance were given through the medium to members of the sparse congregation and then at last she pointed in my direction and I well recall her message: 'There is a wonderful golden light all around you – you are a healer. Yes you – the lady in the blue hat.' She was pointing at one of the ladies sitting in front of me, the lady in the blue hat, who appeared totally surprised by this information because she kept turning to her friend and whispering with raised eyebrows. I slumped behind, disappointed that this much-desired message was not for me. 'Yes, you must listen' continued the medium, 'you will only have to go into a room to make a person feel better. You must get on and heal.' Fortunately, it was not too long before I realised the guidance had been meant for me after all. What the lady in the blue hat did with it is unknown but this event gave me a useful insight into one of the possible pitfalls of platform mediumship.

After a few more visits I plucked up courage and enquired about helping with the healing sessions at the Church on Wednesday afternoons. The person in charge introduced me to their healer, an elderly lady of generous proportions whose legs were tightly encased in elastic bandages. Mrs Dearly, as I will call her, told me 'They don't like healing in the Church itself – it upsets the vibrations' and led me to a sparsely furnished side room that smelt of damp. Still, it had a decent treatment couch and I liked the familiar framed print on the wall of Jesus with the little children around him. One or two regulars came to the weekly afternoon sessions but not many new patients crossed the threshold so Mrs Dearly had time to instruct me. For example, she explained that the practice of flicking her hands towards a corner of the room while healing was throwing away the negative energy, which the spirit people would come and dispose of later. The spirit people also came at night to read requests for absent healing that people had written in the book on the side table. Well-intentioned though these sessions were, I confess to wondering how long I would continue to make the tiresome bus journey into town every week and get home again in time to meet the boys from school. Needless to say, my purpose in being there had yet to become clear.

One afternoon Mrs Dearly greeted me with the information that a husband and wife she knew would be coming along later to meet me. She had apparently met this couple, James and Pam, while out shopping and had told them she had a new young lady assistant who she thought lived near them. This information was of great interest because this elderly couple of Spiritualists had recently been talking about how nice it would be to have someone else to sit with them at their home, when a disembodied voice in the room said 'She's on your doorstep.' They immediately began a mental tally of all the possible females in their little village and even tentatively approached the most likely one, but all in vain. The meeting with Mrs Dearly therefore raised their hopes and brought them to the Church where we discovered that we lived just a few miles apart in adjoining villages.

My home situation at this period was less than ideal and I was grateful for the new friendship with James and Pam. I particularly missed my dad and so his occasional letters, often enclosing a five-pound note, meant a huge amount to me. I did my best to pursue my healing development at home and a couple of incidents spring to mind. The first was when I was lying in bed asking for absent healing for someone who I had been told was very ill, when (another) disembodied voice told me 'He died yesterday' and indeed I later learned that he had. I have never found such experiences scary because they bring with them a sense of calm and ordinariness. I find them interesting rather than sensational. However, such direct psychic experiences were, and still are, quite rare for me.

The second incident concerned my younger son, Stuart, who showed me lumps that had appeared under his feet and even under a couple of toenails, which I took to be verrucas. Naturally I saw my chance and offered healing but he replied, 'No, I want to go to the doctor's like other boys.' The doctor confirmed the diagnosis and explained to Stuart that these were a kind of wart that could be treated at the clinic although there was a nine week waiting list and he concluded the interview by saying, 'I think you'd better go home and let mummy deal with them.' Triumph! So Stuart had a few healing sessions on his feet and stopped complaining about the pain. However, when he later showed me that all the verrucas had turned black I was horrified, thinking something awful had happened to them. Fortunately, a friend arrived at that very moment and explained that this is what happened when verrucas are treated chemically and they were now dead and could be easily removed, which proved to be the case.

I began to visit my new friends in the adjoining village one evening a week, sitting in their neat bungalow in silent session or listening to their experiences and sometimes exchanging healing. They were followers of the Silver Birch teachings that were channelled through the mediumship of a former agnostic, Maurice Barbanell, who also founded The Psychic News, the most popular and respected newspaper of its kind. I had no difficulty in embracing the gentle wisdom of these Teachings, which I found both helpful and comforting in my everyday life. James and Pam also had a fund of recorded cassette tapes including many through the renowned direct-voice medium, Leslie Flint, some of which I found quite interesting and others so mundane I wondered why the communicator had bothered. Evidence of life after death is one thing, but even at that stage in my journey I questioned the point of an afterlife if it was just some improved replica of the one they had left behind, complete with rose-covered cottages and cups of tea.

James himself was a medium and we often had guidance from a spirit person they called 'the Doctor' who spoke in a kind but authoritative voice that seemed much bigger than suited James's slight frame. I had healing from the Doctor on several occasions and one evening he told me that my backache was due to poor posture and that I should sleep straighter and not curled up in the foetal position. This is easier said than done when you are asleep, of course. However, I was violently awoken one night shortly afterwards by what I would swear was a pair of cymbals being clashed loudly above my head, causing my body to straighten out like a tin soldier. The next occasion was gentler, this time sounding as if my pillow was filled with something like dried hops that were being rubbed together against my ears. It was strange but comforting to know that my invisible friends were concerned for me.

As I sat opposite James in the muted light of their sitting room one evening, I thought I could see him changing shape, growing even smaller and curving forward in his chair. Fascinated, I dropped silently to my knees and crept up to get a better look, whereupon the face of an old Chinese man turned to look directly at me and with a broad grin chuckled, He! He! He! This entity and Pam then had a conversation like old friends and I had another experience of transfiguration mediumship.

The GP doctor who had given Stuart advice on his verrucas was immensely caring when my husband fell down a flight of stairs at work and suffered a serious, though mercifully not permanent, head injury. The months of caring for him at home, fighting an industrial tribunal case on his behalf and trying to keep some sense of normality for the children were dark and difficult for me and yet punctuated by demonstrations of great kindness from friends. Being an intelligent, determined and physically strong man, my husband used his slow convalescence to study for a new qualification that ultimately led to him setting up his own highly successful business. But the strains of the intervening years finally snapped the already frayed threads of our relationship and we parted on amicable terms, both keenly conscious of the need to minimise the impact of our separation on Michael and Stuart.

Within a short time my husband inherited sufficient funds to buy a pleasant flat a few miles away whilst the boys and I remained in the rented cottage. I had a part-time job driving vans and delivering meals to the elderly but needed more income to survive. Fortunately, I managed to secure an administrative position at a college of art and design. I was still in my 30's, slim and reasonably attractive, and now in the kind of environment that I had never encountered before, although I had long aspired to. Just the thought of attending art school was outside anything in my upbringing and so to be in that setting now, even in a support role, was a delight, for the pursuit and appreciation of art has always been important to me. This is why I felt irritated by the few students who abused what I thought of as a privilege.

When the opportunity arose to train in-house as a student counsellor I jumped at it, probably imagining myself as some kind of Florence Nightingale of student psychology. The first question our tutor asked our little group was 'Why do you want to be a counsellor?' We thought this was a strange thing to ask because obviously, we replied, we want to help others. 'No' she stated firmly, 'it's because you are damaged.' What was she talking about? I had the feeling this wasn't going to be what I'd signed up for.

In reality, the training brought me head-on with painful emotional and mental challenges that taught me a great deal about myself. Foremost amongst these revelations was what appeared at the time to be a powerful aversion to male dominance, targeted at an unfortunate and completely blameless tutor who had taken over from his female colleague half way through the course. One day this man simply asked us to draw a picture of our group. My drawing depicted each of the eight students sitting in a circle, which we normally did, but hovering above the group was a truly diabolical representation of our teacher's face, together with long thin hands held before him as if ready pluck us out. It was a deeply disturbing image and no doubt extremely hurtful to the tutor but it seemed to have come from nowhere, as if it had drawn itself. The sheer depth of feelings that accompanied the drawing erupted from within me like a volcano and continued for weeks. They were truly shocking: feelings I did not like and which I'd had no idea existed beneath the surface of my outwardly placid façade. Clearly, we are not who we think we are. Only after many years of searching through buried memories did I discover the possible root of this episode. Fortunately however, I eventually managed to return to the course and the tools of counselling have stood me in good stead in my role as a healer, even if they were really secondary to this experience of self-discovery.

A fellow trainee on the counselling course was a warm-hearted lady named Rene, who was nearing retirement from her post as head of textile design. We were having lunch at her delightful art-filled home one day while I was telling her how the children and I were being harassed by the new landlord who wanted us out of the cottage in order to rent it at a considerably higher premium. A friend had told me of a house that was for sale by a charity at a reasonable price but I was unable to raise the full deposit. Rene turned and casually said, 'I'll lend you the money' and I burst into tears over my soup. That single act of generosity brought a positive change of life for the boys and me and we at last moved into a home of our own.

By this time, James and Pam had moved away but remained in touch. James's son Jon had recently re-trained and taken a job near our new house but his wife and daughter had to remain some distance away until they found a buyer for their property and so Jon became a weekday lodger for a while. Whilst he was not a full trance medium like his father, Jon certainly had psychic abilities and we would spend some evenings sitting in session to see if we could get any 'messages'. I have to confess that most of these were pretty banal and the kind of stuff most people could come up with if they thought hard enough, although words about the cancer of greed spreading like poison across the planet were true enough. After a while though, and perhaps because we were setting our sights higher, we received a couple of communications that would prove to be significant: I was told that I would be guided in the work I was to do and that I would work with 'Zed'. This word meant nothing to us; we didn't know if it was the name of a person or a philosophy or something else and searches through books (these were the days before home PCs and search engines) proved fruitless and so the message was written down and put out of mind. Strangely, because I assumed that my spiritual role was that of healer, I was also told that I was to 'prepare the way for someone who was to come'. I can't recall the exact words but it sounded very biblical.

I continued to practice my healing whenever possible as the boys continued their education and grew into beautiful, witty young men in spite of my parental shortcomings. I changed my job to a position aptly described in a poem by John Betjeman: 'I am a young executive, no cuffs than mine are cleaner, I have a slim-line briefcase and I use the firm's Cortina.' My briefcase was black and my Ford Cortina was new and white and replaced a long succession of unreliable motors, some of them purchased from the local scrap yard. The area of work in which I was most interested, and therefore relatively successful, was that of helping to provide supportive housing for adults with special needs.

Fighting a cause for others is not difficult, especially when you ignore the practical details.

Enthusiasm and force of personality overrode my lack of training to a certain degree but over the years I slid inexorably into the trap of over-confidence, probably bordering on arrogance. With the benefit of hindsight, these unfortunate traits were exacerbated by a certain euphoria of freedom coupled with trying to make my way in a male-dominated environment. But conversely, there was also a growing need within me over the years to abandon the world of business and devote myself fully to healing. Finally I set myself a time-limited escape plan and kept to it.

First I manoeuvred myself into a similar job requiring just 4 days a week and based from my home, which allowed me to set a day aside for my healing practice. I also moved house, ostensibly to be closer to the hostel facilities I was now overseeing but this also had the additional advantage of freeing me from my perceived function as local agony aunt cum soup kitchen. The process of selling and seeking houses was both interesting and frustrating and just when I was at the point of giving up, details of an attractively shabby bungalow arrived in the post and I knew my months of searching were over even before I set foot over the threshold. Confirmation that this was the right place came when I returned from the viewing to find an offer for the purchase of my house waiting for me. The house Rene made possible had been my refuge and security: the next one was to be my haven of peace.

My new house was in a neglected and sorry state with a large overgrown garden but I was delighted with it. My friendly surveyor was clearly worried on my behalf and advised me that I could buy a brand new, ready-to-go house on an estate for the same money. He may have thought I was unwise but I thought he was short-sighted, for no amount of fresh paint and fitted kitchen units could equal my airy rooms and sea views and although it took around 20 years to carry out all the urgent repairs and improvements it needed, that process was enjoyable too. Family and friends arrived in the early days to help make the place liveable; ancient wiring and plumbing were corrected, a proper sink and cooker installed, doors made to fit, knee-high grass cut down and the first vegetables planted. For a girl whose childhood had been spent in the lower half of a terrace house with no horizons, this was heaven.

The volume of work and throughput of visitors took their toll though and within months of moving in I contracted the shingles virus with an unsightly rash that spread from the centre of my chest and down my right arm to my fingers. Desperate for some pain relief, I finally found a local doctor who came and sat on my bed and, after confirming that I had a bad case of the shingles, talked at length about healing until I reminded him that I was in pain (I am not averse to medical intervention when necessary). Finally he rummaged in his bag and produced a couple of foil-wrapped tablets, one of which I tore open and stuffed into my mouth the moment he left the room. Unfortunately it was the water-soluble type that filled my mouth with foam and a dreadful taste. However, I was able to register with this friendly doctor and it proved to be a contact that would lead to other unexpected developments.

Until then I had not been very interested in therapies but this illness was to open my eyes to their possibilities. Firstly, a kind friend who practised a kind of divination concluded that I was deficient in zinc and that I needed a particular Homeopathic remedy, which certainly seemed to help. After a month or so I was able to leave my bed but I still felt ill and utterly devoid of strength and therefore unable to return to my paid employment. It was then that an acquaintance who was studying for a qualification in Homeopathy asked if he could 'take my case', i.e. practise on me, which he began by asking questions for about an hour and a half. I was not really surprised when the first remedy he prescribed seemed to have no effect and so wasn't exactly excited when the second attempt arrived in the post. Inside the envelope were two little tablets with the instructions to take one and leave the other until we had spoken. I popped the tablet into my mouth, rose from my desk, walked halfway across the room and was stopped mid-stride by an invisible wall. Even at the time I recall thinking that it was like something from a Tom & Jerry cartoon when the cat gets stopped in its tracks by the mallet on the head. Suddenly I was completely and utterly exhausted: all I could manage was a left turn into the bedroom where I threw myself onto the covers and slept for 15 hours, broken only by necessary trips to the bathroom and occasional cups of tea. But this was not a one-day effect, for the pattern of unnatural periods of sleep, day and night, continued for weeks and I was physically unable to do anything but to go with it. The trainee Homeopath had hit the nail on the head with his diagnosis: exhaustion. The whole of the summer disappeared before I could return to work but the interesting point of this experience was that the remedy was not a 'quick fix' but the identification and treatment of the very cause of the problem. Much like spiritual healing, in fact.

After completing the commitment I had given of 2 years in the part-time job, I left behind the salary, the car and the pension scheme, the expenses and the status, and stepped into a life of financial insecurity and spiritual openings. It felt wonderful.

Up to that point I had refused payment for healing, being conditioned by the old school of mainly Spiritualist practitioners who claimed that it was wrong to take money for a God-given gift. This was a prime example of the need to question everything, for how was I to practise healing, pay the mortgage and feed myself if I had no income? Where did vicars stand within such pronouncements? The answer was quite simple: I would charge just sufficient to meet my needs: the issue was not of money but of motivation. Most people were more than willing to pay and yet it was years before I overcame my reluctance to step forward and accept the value of what I did. To those who came I explained that I charged for my time: the healing was free.

What this period of indecision taught me was the central lesson of trust, for however narrow my financial tightrope became at times, the balancing rod of salvation always arrived in the nick of time. For example, an electricity bill arrived one morning and while I was wondering how I would pay it I opened a second letter that contained a cheque for almost the same amount. The cheque was from a client I hadn't seen for some time who wrote that she just felt she wanted to say thank you for the healing she had received. Another coincidence? I think not.

I joined a small 'seekers' group and gradually made friends in the area. One incident perhaps worth mentioning was when I was asked to give a demonstration of healing during one of the regular group meetings. I took up my position at one end of the room with the elderly lady who had agreed to be the subject and although I attempted to tune in the normal way, it felt rather strange. After some minutes of this, the leader of the group who was a respected professional medium, stood up and addressed the assembled group by saying, 'I can see what you're doing and I know who you are and you can stop it now!' Unbeknown to me, another psychic in the back row had decided to put an energy block on the healing demonstration. I never knew whether this was an act of jealously or mischief or something else but thanks to the leader's intervention it provided me with a demonstration of a different kind and fortunately allowed the healing to take place. This was the first, but unfortunately not the last time I would come across unpleasantness from someone professing to be following a spiritual pathway.

Within a short while I set up a couple of meditation and development evenings at my home and more people came to see me for healing, all recommended through word of mouth. I had observed over a period of months that the effects of my healing were changing since devoting myself to it full-time and that clients would often experience far deeper states of consciousness during a session, sometimes aware of a kaleidoscope of colours, the presence of loved ones or even relevant guidance from an inner source. Another effect that happened with increasing frequency over the coming years was 'disappearing time' where recipients would be convinced the healing had lasted just five or ten minutes instead of the forty or fifty it had really been. In fact, some were quite cross at being brought back from their deep state, thinking they had been short-changed. The parallel with my first meditation experience was obvious.

I also began to observe how bodies might perform subtle or even marked self-correcting movements whilst the person remained totally relaxed. One early incident was when I was visiting a lorry-driver who was confined to bed with an injured back. Almost at once his body began to move spontaneously, and without pain he was turned over to lie on his stomach which caused his pyjama jacket to roll further up his back. I then watched in wonder as the muscles around a section of his spine undulated under the skin to realign the vertebrae whilst the rest of his body lay completely still. Like so many people after him, this man spoke of the movements as 'doing themselves'. A physiotherapist I subsequently treated, who was moved into a squatting position and gently revolved with her head on one side, explained it beautifully when she remarked, "This is really weird and I wouldn't have thought of it myself, but I know exactly what it's doing."

'Weird' became the most commonly used word in my healing room over the years as clients related their widely varied experiences.

It was around this time that Bill Hoskins came to see me.

Chapter 4

The people who came to the meetings in my house were of different ages and backgrounds but they all had the same basic desire explore the deeper side of life in the company of like-minded friends. Together we shared our experiences and ideas, some of them meaningful, others quite wacky, but all valid on the road to greater awareness.

One regular at the weekly meetings was a rather quiet lady named Mo who had been aware of a voice speaking to her since early childhood and comforting her when she was punished for 'making up stories'. The first incident she can recall is when she was just 18 months old, looking down from ceiling height at her little body in the cot and her mother sitting beside it because, as she learned much later, she was seriously ill at the time. In her late teens and early twenties Mo was guided to learn more about her natural talents with two experienced mediums who lived a considerable distance from her home. For a year or so Mo made the journey to these sessions that involved taking 3 trains there and 3 trains back again. Finally she was advised that she had achieved the basic understandings of the work and could continue her training by attending a Spiritualist Church closer to her home. Strangely though, she did not feel drawn to the one closest at hand but travelled on to the next where she felt comfortable 'sitting in circle'.

The medium in charge of this circle centred the training on controlling the mind so that it would not interfere with the observation and transmission of incoming information. It is obvious that without such training the mind will impose its own conditioned interpretation of what it receives psychically, and unfortunately this is a trap that many with such latent abilities unwittingly fall into. However, after 5 years of dedicated work and practice as a medium and speaker, Mo felt guided not to pursue this particular avenue and walked away, but not before being given an indication of her future role and coming to know the beings who shared her journey.

The intervening years were busy with moving to a new area, the birth of 3 children and employment. Eventually though, Mo began to experience the need to resume her spiritual work, responding to what is known as an 'inner command', but she didn't want to return to the Spiritualist Movement and had no idea where else to start. The solution came when her postman husband delivered a healing magazine to a lady who happened to be in her garden hanging out the washing. He told her 'My wife is interested in this kind of thing' and through this contact with my friend Carol, Mo duly became a member of the group where her psychic abilities coupled with a kind heart became invaluable supports for me and others while her own spiritual work came to fruition.

By now my own background had provided me with some insight into the fields of psychic perception and although I still had much to learn I was beginning to realise the importance of an open mind firmly coupled with a healthy scepticism. Along the way I had sometimes been attracted by fringe areas like personal prediction but even these had a purpose in that they showed me where I didn't want to go. Spiritual healing was always my mainstay but I knew that what I call spiritual mediumship was also part of the divine picture.

At this stage in the narrative it seems sensible to offer a basic understanding to readers who have little or no direct experience of such things, especially as the subject of mediumship was to play an even greater role in events.

The explanation begins with the premise that the soul, or being, progresses through different dimensions or 'bands' of energy, vibrating at increasing frequencies. The place of souls within these bands is governed by the amount of spiritual awareness they have gained thus far and is therefore fluid. This obviously embraces the concept that each of us has a soul that can exist independently of the body, which in turn suggests a continuation of life after death – and also an existence before this lifetime. Materialists rooted in the belief that there is nothing beyond this physical life will find such statements challenging and it is neither my purpose nor wish to persuade them otherwise for we must all come to our own conclusions. Die-hard materialists are unlikely to have read this far anyway. However, what is proposed here is that life itself is a continuous spiritual experience, even though our everyday perception of it is limited to the physical dimension and linear time. An image that has always appealed to me is that of individual pearls (lifetimes) strung upon a single thread (the spiritual journey).

It is a fact that after thousands of years and across the range of cultures and religions, the phenomenon of mediumship is little understood, even by those who practice it or witness it at first hand. The reasons for this lack of clarity are fairly obvious to any objective researcher so the aim here is to try and bring the reality of mediumship into its place in the 21st century and beyond. In essence, the word 'mediumship' denotes communication between dimensions of existence and a 'medium' is the physical part of the exchange.

That is the basic definition but it is absolutely essential to know that mediumship and mediums are on different levels of competence and awareness, as are spiritual healers and teachers. It is also very important to understand that mediumship is an inherent spiritual ability within certain individuals that may be developed but not acquired, and a medium is able to reach dimensions only up to the level of awareness that his/her own soul has gained, for they would be unable to bear frequencies above that. For this reason it is possible to see that a person may be an excellent medium in terms of contact and yet what is conveyed through that channel may or may not be of great spiritual value.

There are basically two types of mediumship: semi-trance and full-trance.

In the semi-trance state, the medium is able to attune themselves to a non-physical source so that information can be received and passed on whilst their mind is still awake and conscious of what is going on. The information may come clearly, either audibly or visually, or as symbols or impressions to be interpreted, and may include the psychic equivalent of the other senses of touch, taste and smell. It therefore follows that the more untrained and conditioned the mind is, the more likely it is to put its own interpretation on the communication, however honest and well intentioned the individual may be. Like my friend Mo, an aware medium will understand this and adopt a dedicated training to avoid this pitfall, often taking years of regular meditative practice to quieten the everyday mind and deal with aspects of their personality that might be a hindrance to keeping a clear channel. They will know that natural ability is not enough on its own and that an undisciplined mind that knows only what it has absorbed since birth will quickly lead them into realms of the imagination.

As previously mentioned, many semi-trance mediums work within the Spiritualist Movement in the U.K. and elsewhere, where the emphasis is on gaining evidence of the survival of the personality beyond death which mediums provide through messages for individuals in the congregation (e.g. 'the lady in the blue hat') or on a one-to-one basis, mostly from deceased family and friends. The mediums are usually clairaudient, hearing the messages and passing them on, or clairvoyant, seeing the discarnate person, or both. It is not unusual for semi-trance mediums to also be impressed by the communicator's energy so that they briefly experience particular feelings or even symptoms of an illness that are relevant in terms of 'evidence' such as, 'I'm getting a pain in the chest – did this person have a heart condition?'

The mind of an advanced semi-trance medium could be likened to a sports commentator who watches and reports on the action of a match without adding his or her own opinions. This more objective approach is especially likely when the medium works in partnership with an active spirit personality, or 'guide', and valuable counsel as to the choices that may face an individual is often given through this means. The familiarity of such a relationship also helps the medium to relax and trust the process and sometimes allows a set of teachings to be built up over time. Such partnerships are forged beyond the medium's current incarnation and are understood to be part of interweaving experiences extending back through many varied lifetimes within a group or 'family' of souls.

The state of full-trance mediumship is far less common than semi-trance and requires great spiritual discipline and the complete surrender of mind, which is surely the greatest test of all. Once again it is important to stress that this is an ability the person was born with and although it may be helped to develop, it is not some technique that can be acquired through study or practice and especially not from attending a few weekend courses. The medium in the full-trance state has moved beyond their conscious mind and is at one with their higher self, i.e. the part of them that is not restricted to physical existence. It therefore follows that their mind is not conscious during the ensuing experience and so they are unlikely to have any memory of it afterwards. In other words, they are working to their highest frequency level to blend with and allow selected spirit beings to use their physical body as a vehicle for communication. This may manifest in a variety of ways.

The medium entering the full-trance state will probably appear to relax and fall asleep, although often there will also be changes in breathing and posture as the 'communicator' takes over. More difficult to describe is the change of energy and 'presence' in the room when this occurs. The communication may simply be through speech, with the voice of the personality being either impressed on the medium's own manner of speaking, or may sometimes be the voice they used whilst in a physical form, so the novice observer may be startled to hear a male voice speaking through a female medium and so on. Communicators may sometimes speak in a language that is foreign to the medium, sometimes one of ancient origin that requires lengthy research to decipher, and one assumes this is to provide some veracity of the channel.

More unusually, communicators may utilise the body as well as the voice of the medium and make their former physical appearance apparent, as in the cases of my friends Tony and James. This kind of mediumship is called 'transfiguration' and, as I said before, it has to be seen to be believed. This usually happens with the medium's normal appearance gradually assuming that of the incoming personality, rather like the computer technology of morphing. I recall holding a session of group dynamic healing at a workshop in Leicester some years ago and noticing the features of an elderly gentleman gently morphing from one face to another. He confirmed afterwards that he was a medium, although he had been unaware of anything but the healing during the session.

A rare manifestation of full trance that has been documented, investigated and frequently derided though not disproved, is that of physical, or material, mediumship where the medium appears to exude a kind of dense energy that independently adopts a recognisable human form. These energy forms may be fairly insubstantial or may progress to flesh-and-blood appearance and converse with and be touched by people in the room before returning to their own dimension via the medium who remains seated in full trance. Cases of trickery at the turn of the 19th century do not account for the rigorously tested mediumship of Helen Duncan and other physical mediums, any more than the disbelief of those who have not experienced the phenomenon makes it an unreality. We must hope that as humankind moves further into this age of quantum physics it will allow itself to be more open to those experiences which, although as yet unmeasured, are honest, valid and potentially life changing.

Helen Duncan was a Scottish housewife and physical medium who was one of the last people to be prosecuted in England under the 1735 Witchcraft Act that amazingly was still in force in the 20th Century. Helen was well known in Spiritualist circles and gave great comfort to many bereaved people, especially during the time of the Second World War. In a now infamous trial in 1944, Helen was accused of being 'a witch and spy guilty of revealing wartime secrets' by an Old Bailey jury in London because of potentially sensitive information she had disclosed in the naval city of Portsmouth, 'allegedly via contacts with the spirit world'. This 'sensitive information' related to detailed messages from recently deceased sailors being given to their loved ones through Helen's mediumship *before* the Government had released information that the ship on which they were serving, the HMS Barham, had been sunk. Shamefully for British justice, Helen was found guilty and imprisoned in Holloway Gaol for nine months. It was largely as a consequence of this farcical trial that the Witchcraft Act was repealed in 1951 and replaced by the Fraudulent Mediums Act. Unfortunately, this new legislation was used to continue to hound Helen, who died in 1956 shortly after a police raid on premises where she was sitting in trance. It is said that the sudden withdrawal from trance caused her to bleed internally.

The danger of sudden disturbance to anyone in a state of full trance is well established and Helen Duncan was not the only medium to be seriously injured through shock or physical contact. Another famous physical medium of that era was Alec Harris, a devout Welsh Christian and former sceptic who used to be tied to a chair in the trance state whilst substantial spirit forms emerged via the energy he produced and walked amongst the audience, talking, greeting and even embracing them. One account tells how Sir Alexander Canon had conversations with two materialised Tibetans in their own language, whilst on another occasion a professor of classics spoke with a spirit form in ancient Greek. Equally significant though were the thousands of bereaved folk who were able to plainly see, touch and be comforted by loved ones they had previously thought of as dead. So whilst these sessions brought great joy to those present, there were plenty of outsiders convinced they must be employing some kind of trickery. Alec's wife Louie records that while they were living in South Africa, a group of journalists intent of exposing the 'fraud', interrupted a demonstration by suddenly grabbing one of the spirit forms and simultaneously taking flashlight photographs and pulling down the curtains. We can assume the journalist had a nasty shock when he found himself with empty arms, but unfortunately this was nothing compared to the damage done to Alec Harris, who from that day on was too ill to work or even function normally for the remainder of his life.

Another piece of information in Louie's subsequent book that became significant to me later on was how she was told early on in Alec's development, 'Your man is like the engine. You are the power which makes the engine go.' In other words it was to be a spiritual partnership with each playing their unique part.

A surprisingly large number of people are not mediums but have some degree of psychic ability. The term 'psychic' or 'sensitive' is given to someone who has a developed faculty of non-physical perception through their parallel non-physical senses of sight, sound, smell, taste and touch. Some psychics are mediums and some are not. Psychic tendencies are, like mediumship, sometimes apparent from early childhood and sometimes develop later in life, but how they are expressed (or suppressed) is unique to each individual. Many children are psychically awake until life's conditioning or sceptical adults close their minds, whilst others have the benefit of a more open and nurturing upbringing.

Many people, if not most, have at least one spontaneous psychic experience in their life, even if they are reluctant to speak of it. They may see or sense the presence of a loved one, smell an old familiar perfume, hear their name called, know the moment a friend has died or suddenly be aware of a warning of a future event: the list is long. In simple terms, these occasional experiences may be likened to a window opening to reveal a scene from a different dimension and time.

It must be said that psychic ability in itself does not necessarily denote great spiritual awareness but it can be a very useful tool in gaining it. One of the greatest dangers in the world today is the desire for sensationalism and the gullibility of otherwise sensible people when it comes to psychic matters. Of course I accept that some of my own work may seem sensational, and in terms of it being amazing and outside normal experience it sometimes is. Sensationalism, though, is about reacting to an experience with imagination or desire and making more of it than it warrants. The truth is that spiritual experiences seek neither status nor admiration and spiritually aware minds know this to be so.

Some spiritual healers, like Harry Edwards and Mo, are also psychically gifted but others, like me, are not. I believe that we choose how to utilise these talents before we enter a lifetime and therefore making judgements on ourselves or others is a waste of time. There is, however, a basic truth that every human being needs to know and it is this: each and every one of us is a spiritual being temporarily clothed in physical form and each and every one of us has a direct link to spiritual wisdom and guidance. That link is within us and can be found through the inner pathway of meditation.

As I said, I coined the title 'dynamic healing' to try and describe the phenomenon of spontaneous and involuntary self-correcting movements that were happening in response to my energy. The healing itself was no different in terms of anything I had said or done previously and yet I often found myself clearing the floor of furniture and standing well back as clients, as I call them, went into action. It is important to make it clear that not everyone responds with movement because obviously it may not be appropriate for any number of reasons.

By 1987, news of my healing work was spreading and a local newspaper article mentioned that some patients were referred to me by their doctor (actually the same one who had given me the foaming pain-killer). Shortly after this I received a brief handwritten note from the chairman of a healing organisation I had never heard of, demanding the name and address of the doctor. I later learned that this was for a research programme but I have to say my response was also brief and to the point. It eventually transpired that this was yet another link in the chain of unexpected events. A more measured letter then arrived explaining that this was an umbrella organisation potentially for all healing groups that aimed to develop a code of conduct for healers that would be acceptable to the medical profession and the E.E.C. This was just the kind of legislation I was then opposed to and so I gladly accepted the invitation to meet in London.

At this time there were moves to regulate and register all therapeutic practitioners, mainly to protect the public from charlatans, but I was dismayed to see that healing had been included in this. My objections lay in the simple principle that spiritual healing is just that – a spiritual interaction and not a therapy that may be learned from books and practised for a given result. Spiritual healers work intuitively: they do not diagnose or prescribe, they do not manipulate and seldom touch, and so what is the point making them learn anatomy and physiology? And who would dare put themselves forward to quantify a person's healing power? I decided to apply to join the largest healing organisation, The National Federation of Spiritual Healers, to try and have a voice from the inside. With backing from the chairman of the umbrella organisation, my application was accepted and I discovered that the hierarchy of established healers within the organisation actually supported the legislation because they believed it would give them status and take them a step closer to working within the National Health Service. They even continued to encourage healer members to wear white hospital coats.

However, that trip to London had another spin-off in that I gave the chairman healing at his request and his reaction was so violent that he almost fell off his chair. The interesting point was not the dynamic reaction but the fact that it didn't surprise him. It transpired that he was friendly with another healer who also had this dynamic effect on her clients and it was therefore not a new experience for him. I was intrigued because I had not heard of other dynamic healers either in the UK or elsewhere in the world. I then learned that the organisation's researcher at that time was an American psychiatrist named Daniel J Benor, who went on to write the most comprehensive study of spiritual healing research ever published. Dan knew of two other dynamic healers and subsequently arranged a meeting between the three of us: a lady in London, a healer by the name of Ron Staley who came from Staffordshire, and me.

We met in the home of the first healer, Addie Raeburn, a former Olympic skier married to Major General Sir Digby Raeburn, one time Governor of the Tower of London and a supporter of complementary medicine. Addie was hugely entertaining and down to earth in her accounts of her healing practice and related how, as I have often found myself, clients sometimes perform such amazing postures that neither they nor their healer can help breaking into fits of laughter! Addie was still in her teens when she became aware of her ability to heal whilst caring for her sick aunt. Later on she discovered that her healing was effective in combination with the massage she used to treat the injuries of fellow skiers. At the time of our meeting she was offering healing to individuals from a range of social backgrounds as well as taking part in a number of healing research projects. The highly impressive effects of Addie's healing on people and animals are well documented by Daniel Benor and others.

By contrast, Ron took a quieter and perhaps more reverential approach. He had come across spiritual healing while seeking relief for his first wife's painful rheumatoid arthritis, which in turn led them to the local Spiritualist Church where she benefited from regular healing until her sudden death two years later. No doubt moved by his grief and loneliness, friends encouraged Ron to return to the Church where he repeatedly received messages telling him that he was a healer and he needed to 'get on with it'. So Ron began tentatively healing at the age of 56, and after remarrying a few years later became firm friends with the priest of his new wife's local Anglican Church who proved to be a great supporter, even inviting Ron to accompany him on his parochial rounds to the sick and encouraging him to establish his own healing practice. It came as a great shock, however, when three years later a seriously injured lady suddenly went into powerful self-correcting movements before his eyes. Reading Ron's account of this first dynamic session, I was struck by its parallel with my own experience with Bill Hoskins: the industrial accident resulting in severe spinal injury and restricted mobility, the inability of medical intervention to correct the condition or significantly relieve the suffering, the dramatic and painless physical response to healing and the immediate cessation of pain and return to full movement. Not to mention the amazement of the healer, of course.

But the one thing I remember most from this meeting was the story Ron told us about being called to the home of a lady who needed help. He said that he was becoming quite well known by this time and walked up to the lady with the words, "Don't worry my dear, we'll soon put you right." He held his hands over her – and nothing happened. After a minute or two he realised what he had done and turned, walked to a corner of the room and went down on his knees and prayed, "Forgive me, Lord: Thy will be done, not mine." He then returned to the patient and the healing flowed. Oh that all healers would have such humility!

Both Addie Raeburn and Ron Staley regularly gave simultaneous healing to small groups of patients with no noticeable lessening of individual results. Addie felt it necessary to be in physical contact with each member of the group and described with much humour how she would spread-eagle herself across the floor to keep a hand on one and a toe on another – reminiscent of a certain children's parlour game. Ron on the other hand (so to speak) did not find physical contact necessary, as neither did I in the years to come.

The other known dynamic healer in the UK before then, though not known to me, was the former physical training instructor and blacksmith, John Cain, who used to hire a local hall for regular group healing sessions in order to deal with the large numbers of people seeking his help. It is well reported that the majority of his patients would spontaneously enter altered states of consciousness, sometimes waking with no memory of what had taken place, even if this had involved physical movement. John Cain was a man of strong opinions, seemingly unconcerned with seeking the source of his ability and with little time for the old school view of healing or the psychic bigwigs of the day. What he did was to work tirelessly for those who sought his help in the way that was natural to him. He died in 1985 at the age of 54.

Unlike John Cain, I have a need to *know*. If I am asked to explain what I do, I now reply that you cannot understand healing unless you understand life, for they are one and the same. Of course, I had no idea back then that I would become the custodian of universal teachings of worldwide importance that would provide the answers to so many of my questions.

Meanwhile, I began to hold healing workshops, sometimes with others and later on my own. This was not a role I slipped into comfortably and I usually felt sick with nerves beforehand and exhausted afterwards. Things were better once I learned to do my preparation and then discard the notes.

The National Federation of Spiritual Healers had been formed in the 1950's by the great Harry Edwards to be an alliance of healers of any philosophical persuasion coming together to promote healing and present a united stand against the critical attitude of orthodox religion and medicine. In its early days healers were joining at the rate of over a thousand a year. There is no doubt that it worked quite well as an alliance but it seemed by the time I became a member that there was confusion regarding the very basic understanding of what spiritual healing actually is. Indeed, the NFSH magazine once invited readers to send in their opinions on the nature of healing, which I thought was a very strange thing for a semi-professional body to do and begged the question as to how it could represent its membership to the outside world when it lacked clarity itself. With hindsight though, even a jumble of differing beliefs is preferable to creating another dogma.

The policy of the Federation at that time was for aspiring members to serve a two-year probationary period under the guidance of a sponsor who would be an existing member. At the end of the period the sponsor would put the probationer forward for full membership, accompanied by testimonials from two satisfied 'customers' and a certificate would then be issued. In due course I became a sponsor for quite a few of the people who attended my workshops in the local NFSH region. I was also fortunate to become friends with the National Chairman at that time, a kindly retired man named Guy Batham, who occasionally stayed at my house en route to visit a cousin, which gave us the opportunity for

48

some in-depth discussions. At Dan Benor's suggestion, I had recently attended a lecture in London on Therapeutic Touch given by Dolores Kreiger from the New York University School of Nursing where this form of healing was taught in conjunction with orthodox nursing. Graduates who wished to utilise their healing ability could then do so quietly and naturally through Therapeutic Touch as they went about their daily duties. It therefore occurred to me that this was an avenue the NFSH might usefully pursue in the UK for spiritual healing. Guy was in favour of the idea and even managed to secure a little funding to produce a healing course for health-care professionals.

Conscious of how such a course might be viewed in professional circles (something that wouldn't bother me now), I invited a former G.P. and current healer member to help write and present it. I also sought advice from a sympathetic nurse-tutor friend who proposed the introduction of carefully selected mentors, something that later became common practice. As far as I recall, the course took place over a certain number of days and weekends and culminated in a written paper and final assessment of the candidate's understanding and suitability as a professional health-care healer. The course was enthusiastically approved by the NFSH Trustees and the first one successfully held for a mixture of medical and therapeutic practitioners. However, the possibility of repeat courses raised an unexpected issue, for this would mean passing my 'baby' over to unknown adopters, each with their own background and beliefs and whilst this may be a good thing on an individual basis, it did not auger well for a standard presentation.

It seems strange now to reflect that the healing course for Health-Care Professionals was the first approved course run by the Federation. My next suggestion was the need for a unified standard for healers wishing to run this course, i.e. training for the trainers, and this in turn led to discussions on the NFSH formulating its own courses for probationers instead of relying on whatever their sponsors

49

chose to pass on. A working committee was formed to draw up a new training course which initially drew on the health-care professionals' material but with omissions and additions according to different viewpoints. I decided to step away before the new course was finalised but at the same time I was pleased that I had perhaps helped to set common guidelines for NFSH healers and their tutors. Whether Harry Edwards would have approved such standardisation is another matter.

At this juncture I had not been in touch with my Art College friend Rene for several years apart from the usual exchange of birthday and Christmas cards and an occasional phone call but out of the blue I had an increasing urge to see her again. We made arrangements and I went to collect her for lunch armed with a huge bouquet of blue larkspur. Then over a pleasant meal I was able to tell her how much her friendship had meant to me at a time when I'd needed it and how her generosity had changed my life. Within just a few weeks of our reunion, Rene had a massive stroke that left her unable to stand, walk or feed herself, and this kind and lively and talented lady subsequently spent the remainder of her years being cared for in a nursing home. I missed being with her when she died by only 20 minutes but at least I had the final privilege of conducting her funeral service.

Chapter 5.

Another person who came to the original group meetings at my house was a consultant surgeon who asked me not to tell the others what he did for a living because he thought this might change their attitude towards him. I thought this was a bit presumptuous but events would prove him right when we arranged for him to observe a couple of healing sessions, with the clients' permission, of course. The first client he saw was someone I knew well and who usually arrived for healing dressed in jeans and a jumper. This day he came in smart trousers, shirt and jacket and if he'd had a forelock I'm sure he would have pulled it.

The doctor, who has asked to be identified as 'John', was more open minded than many in his profession and was also an exponent of martial arts and meditation and therefore well acquainted with concepts of energy. His clinical nurse at the hospital was my friend Valerie, who talked to him about healing in between appointments. One day his telephone rang just as he had taken readings on a patient and so Valerie sat with a comforting hand on the lady until the doctor returned. The readings were then taken again and were so improved that he turned to his nurse and demanded, 'What have you done?' It was after that experience that he asked to join the group.

Valerie had been referred to me by our mutual doctor friend who had been unable to diagnose or relieve the sharp stabbing pains she was experiencing right through her chest. During our healing session Valerie suddenly and dramatically found herself reliving what appeared to be a past-life experience as a young slave girl where her curiosity of a forbidden sacred place had resulted in her being stabbed to death by a guardian priest. This could of course be ascribed to imagination except perhaps that her description of that place and the statue of the deity, which were completely foreign to her present knowledge, were subsequently researched and verified. Her pains also ceased entirely after that session. We were therefore led to the possibility that the trauma of that past experience had surfaced to take her to where she needed to be in the present time.

Valerie's then husband was the chief ambulance officer for the county and he reacted to healing on his back and shoulders in the most extraordinary way. In one memorable session, from a standing position Ian's body leaned forward in a straight line from the ankles up until he stood at an angle of about 45 degrees and yet perfectly relaxed and seemingly balanced. It looked like the trick a clown in his long boots performs and we were almost helpless with laughter. However, the performance was not over because after a while his body straightened up and he then leaned over backwards to the corresponding angle, which is clearly impossible, while Ian declared that he felt as if he was being fully supported 'like sitting in a comfortable armchair.' We always had a good laugh when he was around.

Dan Benor thought it would be good to record some of these dynamic healing experiences and so an amateur video-photographer was found who was willing to oblige. Dr John and Ian were to be the observers and several clients agreed to take part, one of which was a local dumper-truck driver I had seen a couple of times previously who suffered from a painful back condition. With everyone in place in my small healing room, I began the healing and the client went into dynamic action so violently that the shocked photographer could hardly hold the camera steady. For an hour or more in a prone position, the man stretched, undulated and thumped up and down full length so strongly that the heavy wooden couch I had bought second-hand from a hospital warehouse, began 'walking' across the floor. Out of sight of the video frame, the couch was being restrained by a consultant surgeon and chief ambulance officer lying on the floor hanging onto its legs! When interviewed by Dr John afterwards, the man reported that he had felt fine and was only worried that his 'top set' would fall out. It was after this that the fixings on the couch were reinforced with steel bolts.

So how did a highly qualified and respected consultant surgeon respond to this demonstration? Here is his account of his introduction to healing, written in 2012:

"My route to healing from orthodox medicine may be of interest because it is based entirely on *observation* and from *conclusions* drawn entirely on those observations. I do not use 'faith' or 'belief'.

1.   Over 20 years ago I saw an account in a medical journal of a report published by the Royal College of Surgeons of the findings of a group of anaesthetists' visit to China stating that acupuncture relieved significant pain and could be used as a substitute for anaesthesia in surgery. I accepted this because of the source.

2.   Ophthalmic surgeons encounter occasionally a very severe pain for which we have only unsatisfactory and ineffective treatment. This pain has at times lead to suicide, and occurs after shingles including the forehead (post zoster neuralgia). I referred my next two cases to an acupuncturist (a former chief nursing officer) for acupuncture and one was cured whilst the second had the pain converted to a non-painful sensation that she could live with.

3.   The nurse working with me in Outpatients, Valerie, was not surprised at this outcome and disclosed in our brief conversation that she practised 'healing'. I asked if I could watch her sometime and she said it would be better to visit her teacher, Jane Tinworth.

4.   The reason I took the mention of healing seriously was as follows: I was lead inexorably to the following conclusions:

(i) Acupuncture cannot be satisfactorily explained in my view by *our* knowledge of physiology and the body. I discussed this with a pain specialist whom I worked with. This is one 'conclusion' that would be rejected by others. Our 'gate theory' and 'endorphins' in pain experience do not go far enough for the level of pain in (2) above. We in the West believe we have identified all the systems in the body and need merely to fill in the details. Here in acupuncture was a whole system we had missed.

(ii) If in biology we, with our Western approach, had missed something fundamental, what in the full range of reality might we also have missed?

(iii)I was no longer entitled logically to dismiss as impossible something which did not fit into my frame of knowledge.

This was my 'midlife crisis' – unfortunately nothing to do with gorgeous blondes!

5.   The first patient I saw Jane deal with displayed a further *paranormal* phenomenon. This was significant for me as pain relief in itself, at his level of pain, might have been by suggestion, etc. A heavily built, overweight man in a prone position 'bounced' full length repeatedly, several inches from the couch. I noted another phenomenon not in my view explicable.

6.   At a retreat on Iona I was asked to look at a girl in her twenties with a severely sprained and enormously swollen ankle on which she could bear no weight. She could only move about on one leg, supporting herself on the furniture. She had been like this for several days with no improvement. Should she leave the retreat with her mother and cross to Scotland for an X-ray? I spent a very long time examining her and had finally a feeling that nothing was displaced and there was no serious ligamentous disruption i.e. no need for treatment or plastering. This view would be very seriously questioned in the circumstances, justifiably so, and an X-ray would normally be automatic. As I thought what I did, I felt

obliged to tell her, and to re-examine her the next day. The next day there was only a slight swelling and bruising and she was able to walk easily with a slight limp. I was able to confirm my previous impression and she asked her mother, 'Is that man a healer?' which I denied initially. Others present later asked me to help them.

7.   I had to devise some method of trying to help those who approached me. In examining this girl I had no awareness of healing – merely close attention to her ankle: also in this there was some compassion but in all other respects with the 'empty mind' I try to achieve in meditation. I therefore decided to (i) meditate for a while (ii) turn my attention to the person and (iii) meditate again when trying to do what I had been asked to do.

8.   As I later accepted that healing had occurred on Iona, I recognised that 'healing' is a consequence of directed concern rather than an action directed and controlled, such as a surgical operation. I do not seek an explanation as for me intellectual comprehension is not relevant or, as I now think, possible by the conscious mind.

9.   In the subsequent 20 or so years of healing endeavour I came to observe that:

> i. While some striking cures took place, suffering was almost invariably relieved (with the usual failure in bipolar disease) but healing was not necessarily synonymous with medical, i.e. therapeutic cure.

> ii. That healing is independent, or can be, of space and time, i.e. occurs in a plane outside our four dimensional world (3 of space and 1 of time) – a plane I think of as a fifth dimension.

> iii. As relief of suffering is the primary manifestation of healing and not synonymous with medical cure, it follows a pattern beyond our human comprehension but this other sphere is in

our comprehension, compassionate, and a greater reality. This can be phrased as 'God is Love' in conventional terms.

iv. These observations are strikingly in accord with those of others who practise healing.

As will be evident in the above, I was almost dragged into it all, along a route I personally could follow; that is observation and consequent deduction, interpretation. I feel dauntingly privileged to receive the greater insight, by simple observation."

'Dr John' BA FRCS.

Needless to say, there are many whose opinions of spiritual healing are less open than my observer friends and I have met a fair amount of their attacks over the years. One prime example was when I was invited to a discussion on local radio and took along Julie, who is both a healer and a nurse. Chosen from a different viewpoint was a doctor in general practice who I came to suspect was also of a certain religious persuasion but apparently had no direct experience of the subject under discussion. Listening to a recording of the programme afterwards, I feel that Julie and I offered a balanced input on the lines that healing is natural, gives people choice, doesn't seek to conflict with medical advice, and so on, whereas the GP could hardly contain his hostility. The interviewer mentioned that another surgery in the county was reporting good results from having a healer on the staff, with increased symptom relief and a reduction in prescribed medication. He asked the doctor if he would consider having one at his practice, to which the response was, "I would have to be intellectually and therapeutically bankrupt to use a healer!" This was said with such venom that there was a period of silence before the interviewer could gather himself together and continue.

I find it strange that such opponents not only pronounce judgement without any first-hand experience but they also appear completely oblivious of how rude they are being. Another example of this came in a call from the partner of one of my clients, secretly asking me to influence her in a certain matter, which of course I refused to do. In the course of the conversation he told me he thought healing was nonsense but "I don't mind her coming to see you if she thinks it does her some good." Apart from seemingly ignoring the fact that this lady had experienced a dramatic improvement from a chronic debilitating condition, he apparently either had no awareness that he was insulting my integrity or he didn't care.

My son was in his teens when his friend's mother asked him, "Are you aware that your mother is in league with the devil?" Of course, the answer is the same as it was 2,000 years ago so I question how these religious bigots interpret their scriptures. I also wonder if this woman thought she had the right to speak to my child in such a way. Fortunately, Stuart quietly thought she was barmy.

My eldest sister Pamela moved closer to my home and it was a comfort to be able to drive over to see her more often. She told me the reason for choosing her new location was that the new house was in a level area and so it would be easier for her husband to cycle to the shops when she was 'gone', i.e. when she died. This could be considered a strange statement because Reg was significantly older than my sister, but the truth was that she'd always had the feeling she would not live to a great age and we all knew this. An old 78 rpm record of Billie Holliday's 'Gloomy Sunday', a lament on the death of a lover, was one of her teenage favourites that she used to play on our gramophone. This is not to say that Pamela herself was gloomy, for on the contrary she was as funny and outgoing as the rest of the family, but this inner sense and the need for deeper understandings grew as she matured in years. She went to Church and attended healer-training groups and read copiously on spiritual philosophy and psychic and therapeutic subjects whilst caring for her family and working full time in hospital administration. Her husband discouraged her one-to-one healing contacts because he felt they drained her but this did not stop Pamela offering absent healing whenever the need arose and there is no doubt that she was a powerful healer. Then in 1981 she had a life-changing experience that she later wrote down for me:

"About ten years ago I had the 'flu and had to go to bed. One evening I was lying in bed; the light was not on but light was coming through the open door from the landing, when I began to feel very weak and a velvety blackness began to enfold me. I tried to call Reg but no sound came, so I tried to get out of bed. But I could not move even my hand. However, I was not at all frightened; I only thought I would like to be with him.

"The next thing I knew, I was walking across a field of soft springy green turf. Though the velvet blackness was still at each side of me, it had withdrawn to some distance and I walked through clear but soft light. I think I was clothed but had no shoes on as I could feel the cool grass under my feet and the dew coming up between my toes. At the end of the field was a brilliant, glowing light which I knew concealed, or actually was, a person. This person radiated true, absolute, love, accepting me as I was with what I can only describe as selfless loving compassion. As I drew nearer it seemed that He was standing on a low dais or step, and I thought I could see His feet. I was filled with a yearning to be caught up in His love and thought that perhaps He would let me embrace His feet. I had no feeling of humility, only that before such perfect love it would be proper to kneel. Then just before I reached him He said, though I heard no words, 'It is not yet time.'

"I do not remember returning, only being back in bed filled with a great emptiness and longing for Him and with tears, which I was too weak to wipe away, running down my face.

"I haven't been able to describe this experience very well, but since then it has been at the centre of my life. Sometimes, quite unexpectedly, I have a sudden sense, a shaft, of that love and light and I am filled with a joyful longing."

I believe this Near Death Experience had a profound effect on my sister, as NDE's do on virtually all who experience them, for they take away the fear of earthly death and demonstrate the greater reality of life. It is as though we are given a pre-run, a premature glimpse, of what awaits us when we eventually leave our physical form.

Back at home, my doctor friend referred a patient to me who was suffering from acute anxiety and depression. He told him, 'I can only give you pills – go and see Jane.' Whether this was faith in healing or dissatisfaction with medicine is unclear but it transpired that there was undoubtedly some deeper prompting at work. So in November 1987 Malcolm came to my house and I realised I had seen him before at a stall in the local indoor market that he ran with his wife, whom I had also previously met when we had attended the same evening class. He was a tall, powerfully built man in his early forties who was now in a state of terrible tension and insecurity.

Malcolm became a frequent visitor over the next few months as we worked with healing, counselling and relaxation exercises. There were also long telephone calls on most of the evenings he didn't visit, and often when he had. It became apparent over the months that this outwardly materialistic man had a much deeper side and I felt that some of his problems could be due to suppressing this, for I believe there is truth in the Spiritualist philosophy that withholding such abilities can lead to depression.

Malcolm told me that an old friend of his had quite recently introduced him to the basics of Buddhist philosophy and that he had adopted the practice of daily meditation in spite of his illness. It also became increasingly obvious during the healing sessions that Malcolm had a latent but strong psychic ability that produced wonderful colours, bright light and feelings of joy.

An early spontaneous vision during a healing session was of finding himself within a room where shafts of light streamed through a stained glass church window. His attention turned to a table on which a lamp burned, sending its light outwards. On the glass below the window was written 'One Corinthians 13.' Neither of us was familiar with this reference at the time and had to turn to my Bible to find Paul's deeply moving words on love that begin,

'I may speak with the tongues of men or angels, but if I am without love, I am a sounding gong or a clanging cymbal. I may have the gift of prophesy and know every hidden truth; I may have faith strong enough to move mountains; but if I have no love, I am nothing.'

This was to lay the foundation of the work we were to embark upon together for the next few years.

By the beginning of June 1988 Malcolm was clear of medication and actively re-arranging his lifestyle to minimise pressure. Our sessions were becoming more and more interesting as his psychic ability developed and he became increasingly sensitive to energy and particularly the energy within crystals. On more than one occasion I have known him walk into a room and immediately sense the presence of an unfamiliar crystal, no matter how small or well hidden it was.

Not having such psychic talents myself, I had previously been rather dubious concerning the growing fashion for crystal healing and the like until I was confronted with it in a very direct way. Valerie and I were attending a residential NFSH healers' weekend where one of the facilitators gave a short talk on the meaning of crystals. A large table was laid out with all shapes and sizes and colours of crystals and we were told that the way to choose the one that was right for us was to pass a hand over the table and just 'feel' which one we were drawn to. With enormous scepticism, I dutifully passed my hand over the table and suddenly it was actually pulled down with considerable force onto a small pink stone. The facilitator clearly did not share my surprise as I willingly handed over my pound coin and took possession of something that was to become very precious to me. The stone is a piece of unpolished rose quartz about 5cm at its longest and in the shape of a heart – although it was some time before I noticed this fact. Valerie chose an amethyst. Back home in bed the following night I was suddenly awakened by the most peculiar sound and sensation in the room: it was as though something had been tied to a length of string and was being whirled around and around near the ceiling at high speed, creating a rush of air and a low 'whooshing' noise. Gathering my thoughts, I realised that the only thing different in the room was the crystal and that I had not followed the instructions to 'cleanse' it, i.e. to remove any energies it may have picked up so that it could start again 'in neutral'. I took my little stone into the kitchen, put it in a bowl of water and sea salt and went back to bed. I was to learn more about the nature of crystals over the following years, one of the aspects being that crystals are not powerful in themselves but only in response to energies: 'An electric wire with no current is useless and so is a stone with no energy'.

One day as we sat together in meditation, Malcolm relaxed and quickly went into white light whilst continuing to tell me what he was experiencing. He felt himself leaving his body and was able to look down upon his apparently unclothed form bathed in light. He became aware of a lovely but unidentifiable scent, which I directed him to follow to its source. He then felt himself rise up beyond the earth to where he could look down on it and other planets, as in a blue light, and saw them not as matter but as pure energy. At this stage he said a few words as though in wonder such as "Now I see; now I understand." The energy coming from him seemed to expand in force and fill the room. At this point Malcolm spoke in a different tone, deeper and slower than his normal voice but still himself. The voice said, "I have brought Malcolm to you to give you power. He is a reservoir." It said a little more on power and my role that I was too stunned to remember and anyway, I was not entirely convinced at that stage that the message was coming from an 'outside' source. Malcolm himself remembered nothing of the voice and was incredulous. He did, however, feel very good and 'somehow changed' after the session.

The following day Malcolm telephoned to report that he had experienced a strange 'dream' although he had felt awake. He said he was in a wood where the trees were slim and silver and a misty light shone. Again, he smelled the special scent. He came to a clearing where the light shone and a voice spoke to him; deep, male, perhaps a slight accent. The voice told him that I (Jane) would help him develop his power, that the power was for me to use and his role was to help me: he was the reservoir. It said he was not to be a healer himself and he must not use the power for profit or the depression would return. "Jane knows the purpose for which the power must be used. Time is running out."

Malcolm said he remembered thinking, 'If this is really a message and not a dream, I need some proof.' His practise was to meditate for a short period each morning before going to work and so he did this the day after. The meditation was straightforward without, he says, reference to the previous night's vision. He was therefore stunned upon opening his eyes to find the heavy statue of the Buddha, which was kept on a shelf on the opposite side of the room, sitting on the floor at his feet.

By the following week Malcolm was keen and sufficiently comfortable to explore the role of the medium. We sat and relaxed and he went into the colours and light, experiencing great peace and joy, and the power built up until it was almost tangible. The voice came through and spoke to me. "Take the power, you know how to use it" it said, and Malcolm's right hand was offered, palm-out, to mine (this meant I couldn't use the pen and pad I had ready). "Can you feel the power?" it asked. I replied, "Yes, like the energy from the crystals but not the same, stronger." The voice spoke for about five minutes and said: "The crystals are a focus to concentrate the power of thought." I asked, "Where is the source of this energy you bring?" The voice replied, "It is the Ultimate: Malcolm would call it Nirvana, Christians would call it Spirit, you and I call it the Ultimate Energy." It continued, "We have brought Malcolm to you for what you have to do: time is short." I asked, "You say 'we' but who are you and where do you come from?" It answered, "We come from the millennia – from the past and from the future." I had no idea what the 'time is short' meant.

I gave a synopsis of these events to the regular house group at our next meeting and asked Mo if she sensed it was genuine. Mo was quick to affirm and a little later admitted that as we spoke she had been aware of a very tall figure, not really a man but a great *being*, a great presence, clothed in colours brighter and clearer than a rainbow, standing in front of us. This being then followed her around the house until she revealed what she had seen to the group. It made a wonderful impression on us all. As time went on this being, who eventually introduced himself as 'Matthew' but said he was actually a 'collective', played a direct role in Malcolm's psychic development. After some months Malcolm was able to work with him in semi-trance, giving guidance to people on a one-to-one basis. Matthew also partnered Mo in her work with other development groups.

Malcolm and I sat in session weekly and Mo joined us whenever her domestic situation allowed. Within six months Malcolm had reached a level of full trance, although this took him enormous effort and mind control and left him physically depleted afterwards, often shaking and desperate for a drink of water. Mo was able to psychically observe the energy in the room and was told she would be the eyes of the group. She was subsequently given the label 'My Eyes', although the true understanding of this title did not emerge until many years later. My own role was to listen and discuss with the communicator and to record the sessions, which I tried to do unsuccessfully with a tape recorder before moving on to write everything down in longhand. This method was simple in the beginning when the sessions were fairly short but I had to speed up and develop my own kind of shorthand when they later increased in length. However, my impulse to keep accurate records of events was already established by the time of those early sittings, even if the full reason for it took a while to emerge. Not for nothing was I given the title of 'scribe'. Now I am able to draw easily on transcripts that have been safely transferred onto computer, along with more recent material recorded directly onto a device just a few inches square. Hooray for technology!

One day Malcolm's old Buddhist friend gave him a short composition entitled 'About Thought' written by the acclaimed Indian yogi and teacher Selvarajan Yesudian who had founded the famous yoga school in Switzerland with the mystic Elisabeth Haich. This piece really struck a chord with me and was, I feel, another pointer to the direction my own work would take, although like any Truth, there is a wide difference between recognising it and processing it until it becomes an integral part of your own experience. This is the piece:

'If you carry about with you thoughts of ill-will and hatred or anger, their destructive force will tell on your own health of body, your mind and your soul.

The harm they will do you is indescribable.

The Ancients said that thought is the greatest power in the body, more powerful than the word, for it is a transcendental power that infuses the whole world.

Good thoughts, however seemingly unimportant, will not fail to achieve their effects.

Have courage and know that you create your own fate.

Therefore think sound thoughts, such as you would like to see realised at the level of action,

So with perseverance you will soon master your thoughts, which will then help instead of hindering you.

Instead of sowing irresponsible thoughts which poison your own life and that of those you meet, master your thoughts and be aware of the power which you possess.

Then will you come to see the reality of the Great Teacher's Words:

> If matter is mighty, *then thought is almighty.*'

At the beginning of that autumn I received a telephone call with the shocking news that my sister Pamela had been taken ill the previous evening and had died during the night. She was just 58. Needless to say, the shock to the family was enormous. I drove over immediately to be with her husband and their adult daughter and son. There in the living room on the arm of her chair was the book she had been reading the previous evening, open at the chapter headed 'Out of Body Experiences.'

Anyone who has lost a loved one will empathise with the trauma of the following months, and of course my mother never came to terms with losing her first-born. Pamela and Shirley had latterly enjoyed a close friendship and it seemed that Shirley took the loss very hard despite the fact that she could still see and talk to her sister. Shirley admitted that at times when she was in a particularly bad state of grief, Pamela would come to her and say something like, 'Come on silly – cheer up.' When I say that Shirley could see her, I must emphasise that it was seeing Pamela as if she was actually standing there and not some kind of wraithlike apparition. I missed my sister too but it was some comfort to know that Pamela's intuition had prepared her for this transition and I knew she would be back in that place of love and light for which she had yearned ever since her near death experience. Much later I would become aware of her involvement in my healing work.

Meanwhile, Malcolm's psychic development progressed quickly and although his excitement sometimes caused problems, his meditation practice was invaluable in training his mind to be still and stand aside. We continued the discipline of sitting weekly in my healing room and on the 3rd November 1988 something occurred that would take our work to a new level.

The way Malcolm entered the trance state on this occasion seemed different and then a new, softer voice spoke: "Tonight we are establishing a link to a very high plane. The power has to be great and very finely tuned. We are now able to use Malcolm to contact you. Including the earth plane there are seven levels. Before we were at five, now we are moving to a higher level. It will get better as time goes on but at the moment we have difficulty in making contact. As Malcolm's power grows we will be able to converse more freely." There was some personal guidance and then, "Things are coming in the next few months; some you will understand, some you will have difficulty with. It will all piece together eventually."

It said, "Soon you will see the birth of the Golden Age, a time of turning, when mankind will unite in love and harmony, and love is the key. It requires a large number of spiritually aware people to start the process and impart the knowledge and message of love."

The voice told me, "You have great work to do; you do not know how great yet." At the time I wrote the following, 'He asked me to hold my right hand out towards him and as I did so I began to cry. I think that on some level of my being I 'recognised' something.' When I think of it now, I am amazed that I failed to make the connection between the voice that spoke to me then and the being who had come to me long ago and lifted my face and filled me with love.

Finally Matthew came through and gave me instructions on helping Malcolm to return: it appeared that he needed to be 'stepped down' in stages.

Chapter 6.

The same voice came through when we sat the following week. It said:

"There are few mediums who can reach these heights and tune directly into the energy of the cosmos. All that has happened in the past 12 months has been intended for this time.

"Tonight I want to impart three things:
1. a small message for you
2. to the world
3. some time to give you some cosmic power, energy.

"Your work is of vital importance in healing. There is a growing awareness both nationally and internationally and you have a vital role in your teachings and writings. Doors will be opened. I cannot give you details now.

"The urgent message for the world is on ecology. The dispersal of the ozone layers, the evaporation of the rain forests and the effects of the so-called 'greenhouse effect' are the greatest dangers the world has ever faced. Within a decade, if it is not stopped, vast areas of the planet will be dry. You are already seeing reduced grain harvests as a consequence of the higher rise in temperatures. This situation will get worse. The effect will be a shortage of grain on a world basis. The richer countries can survive due to their purchasing power; the third world countries will be unable to do this. The consequences will be disastrous. Urge the world to do something about it. Forces of the universe are concerned at the developments. Heed the warning! That is all I have to say. The importance of the time period cannot be over- emphasised. The politicians talk in terms of decades of safety before anything will happen *but 10 years is the most you have.* That is all."

"Tonight I have something for you; cosmic power. Come forward." I knelt and was given healing.

Matthew then came through to step the energy down again and he and I discussed this new grave warning that implied that unless action was taken by mankind immediately, the planet itself was in danger of dying if the situation was not turned around within the next ten years. He said the Golden Age we had previously been told about would not dawn unless the warning was heeded. When I asked what we could do, Matthew told me to discuss it with Malcolm.

When Malcolm returned from trance state he reported that for the first time he had actually been aware of all Matthew had said, which had been uncanny - like listening to your own voice saying someone else's words. He said he had been 'crumpled up in the corner of the room' until Matthew had picked him up and seated him back in the chair. I had been told the mediumship effort for Malcolm was as if he had run several miles, and this was how he felt. This is some of the advice that was given in the next session:

"He must get used to being a medium and keep in trance for long periods. It would be too much to go into trance for the group though because at our level any interruption could cause a break in communication: like an old crystal set and the whisker jumps. Lower levels are much more basic and easily attained. At this sort of level his heart rate almost doubles and he perspires and loses fluid. The muscle power is tremendous - try and move his arm (I tried and couldn't). Two men could not move his arm. Physical strength is necessary to be totally absorbed in his body and to do this requires the effort of three forces - he, you and me; a trilogy. Mediums do not normally go this high. My terminology is limited because his vocabulary is limited. I am impressing Malcolm to speak. He will never be able to witness our conversations." It also said, "Mediums are required for contacting on different levels for different purposes. Malcolm needs to train for this work like a runner or an athlete needs to train." We were also told that great effort was required on both sides.

Although the ecological warnings were the central issue, I will record a little more on the mechanism of mediumship before moving on. I asked the question, 'This exchange of energy that we do, is it that you need a certain energy in order to be here?' It replied, "I need you as well as Malcolm: it's a combination of the two. The reason I'm stopping and doing that (aligning with my energy, palm-to-palm) is to create a type of harmony to maintain a sort of equilibrium, a stabilisation of the poles. It's difficult to explain in Malcolm's terms. You asked a question of Matthew last time regarding tunes: that puzzled you. Let me explain it this way: a note isn't a single vibration; it's a mixture of vibrations, isn't it? The same applies to the spirit. If it was necessary just to have a single oscillation then you could, in fact, through some specific frequency of power, tune into that. But it's more complex than that; it requires a combination of different waveforms, rather like a tune. After all, if it was just a single waveform, you could get a simple oscilloscope and generate that single waveform and you could tune into a spirit. But it's not as simple as that." I remarked that people have been trying to do this for years and he replied, "It's a good job they can't! It wouldn't make much sense, would it, having a situation where everyone could just contact each other. There must be some order."

On a more personal level we were told, "Eventually, the voice I'm using now will become stronger and much more audible, as with Matthew. But you must understand, Jane, that at this level we are not into gimmicks with accents and we don't wish names, like past leaders, or future ones for that matter. This is an attempt to get some sanity into mankind.

"A New age is emerging. Mediumship, as has existed, has tended to draw from the past to point to the future. What we need is to establish a direct contact between psychically aware people and the entire universe, whole worlds - infinite. There has been a failing on earth of only looking at itself in isolation. The 1990's has to be a universal concept."

'Heed the warning - ten years is the most you have' was a powerful and daunting message to receive and I felt quite overwhelmed. What could I do? What difference could be made by a small group of ordinary people in an ordinary house in one tiny spot on the planet? The responsibility seemed beyond reason.

The main development group continued to meet and send healing to the planet. Malcolm's interest in crystals grew and he began to buy a few from a local shop, selecting them solely by what he sensed they might potentially hold. One day he was intuitively drawn to a large piece of rose quartz that he subsequently smashed into smaller ones to give to each member of the group. It was after this that the following message was given in trance:

19th January 1989: "I have important things for you tonight: conservation and the need to transmit your thoughts throughout the world. The time has now come and I will tell you how it will be done.

"The universe is fifteen thousand million years old. Its initial formation was energy. That energy is still with us today. You, Jane, use it for healing, Malcolm for crystals, and I to come here. It has been known to mankind for several thousand years that crystals can be used with energy. Crystals are one of the basics on which the universe is formed but it is like a tool and has to be used correctly or it is no use. You gave crystals to your friends; some will accept and some will not. Twice a day, morning and evening, hold these crystals and as a group transmit your thoughts to the leaders of the world on the lines I have outlined previously [surrounding them with love]. Continue for several weeks. Conservation has been opened on a world basis. A conference will be called soon and it is important that the right decisions and leadership are shown.

"When you use the crystal, hold it in the palm of the hand tightly and place the stone in your hand in your lap. The base chakras, the red and orange, are directly aligned to the mineral kingdom. That should be enough to ensure a group transmission.

"Thought is a powerful instrument: it can be used for good, it can be used for evil. Everything reacts to thought, *everything*."

Perhaps it is hard for someone now to comprehend the lack of awareness on environmental issues that existed only a comparatively short time ago. As I have tried to explain, even those of us who received these warnings struggled with the immensity of them. After all, the media paid scant heed to the environment and the famines they reported in far-off countries seemed nothing new. Still, we tried to take the message on board and sent our thoughts out as a group, even though we may have felt individually inadequate. It was encouraging when the following words were received on the 3rd March 1989:

"As we said a few weeks ago, a conference would be called and as you are aware, it is happening this weekend. Do not expect great things from this one, but it is a start in the right direction. You have helped directly to contribute to this by all your efforts. But be aware that as you create thoughts of harmony and love, thoughts of protection for the environment, there are individuals and groups that have thoughts of the reverse, motivated by selfish interest, interests of profit: they seek to undo the good that you do. Be aware of that. Be aware also that politicians frequently say things and do not mean them. But with eminently important people like the Royal Family becoming involved in England in the environmental question, public opinion is on the change. The determination of the leadership to do something about this will be decided by public opinion. Carry on the good work. We will speak on this subject again soon. Watch the conference with interest, important points will arise, but remember it is your efforts that will determine the outcome, not mine. We are only there to help. The direction that the planet takes, and that you take in collection of the planet's destiny, is in your hands, not mine. To be any other way would be wrong, because then there would be no purpose in your being here at all."

Just as we had been informed previously, Malcolm had no knowledge of anything that happened when he was in full trance and so it was down to me to relay the information to him afterwards. I gave the title 'Master' to the communicator because that was how he felt to me but this was the response that came a few weeks later: "Do you think it's a good thing to call me 'Master' in front of your friends? A couple have talked and said it is not a good name. As your communications grow in the future and become better known it may be less acceptable. It's a suggestion rather than a direction. I am not saying I prefer no name because here names are essential."

I discussed this with Matthew when he arrived to 'step down' the energy after the session and he suggested that, as this is a question of identity, why not simply call him by a letter of the alphabet, for example, M for Master, P for Prophet? Immediately I chose the last letter of the English alphabet, Z –'Zed'. This was not a conscious decision because the message Jon and I had received some seven or so years previously had sunk rapidly to the bottom of my subconscious mind. I leave readers to ponder over whether the name of Zed had been planted then for further use or whether the informants were aware of the choice I would make in the future. Or it could be neither.

Around this time I asked my nephew John Stubbs, a professional photographer, to take some black and white pictures for a series of articles I was writing on dynamic healing for the 'Caduceus' magazine. He set up the camera and tripod in my healing room and photographed healing sessions with a couple of clients. The results were unusual, if not weird. They appeared to show swathes of energy in a variety of formations around the clients, even to the extent that parts of their physical bodies seemed to have disappeared. The light source in some of the photographs appeared to be coming from the right of the picture even though the actual light from the window was on the left. John was incredulous as he printed them, reporting that even the portrait shots he had taken of me on the beach before the healing sessions showed peculiar light areas around my head and body, and he made repeated checks to make sure there was nothing amiss with his photographic equipment. These photographs were discussed at a group meeting and after his meditation the next morning Malcolm received this message for us both from Matthew:

"Last night you questioned us on how to photograph healing energy as an aid to demonstrate dynamic healing. *Science, as you know it on earth, is that part of mysticism that can be measured.* For 3,000 years energy has been written about by great teachers. In time science will discover how the measurement of healing energy may be achieved but until then investigation is best left. Attempts at photographic demonstrations into healing energy can result in the major part of the investigation being into the method rather than the energy. Critics will always try to demean a demonstration. Write about and practise your healing, Jane. We will open the doors of public acceptance of dynamic healing."

The information coming through the Zed communications was becoming more profound. Personal guidance was given only when it was relevant to the overall spiritual objectives. This was particularly the case with our individual practice of meditation, the key to overcoming the mind's conditioning and opening to the intuitive wisdom within. It was also apparent that this channel had not been created so that great truths could be dictated without question: rather this was an exercise in *spiritual tuition* designed to stretch the receivers to a level where, with sufficient promptings, they could find the Truth for themselves. Zed told us,

"It is right to doubt, it is right to question. Accept nothing, even my presence, without questioning it because only then will you realise the truth, and it is a healthy sign, for anyone who believes blindly is not on the real path at all. The purpose of your presence here is to learn, not just within this room but within this planet. That is why you came. So learn your lessons wisely."

One early example was being asked to consider the nature of transitional thought, which ultimately led to deeper understandings on all kinds of things including the objective of life itself. It became increasingly obvious that we were on the receiving end of extremely important teachings that had to be offered out far beyond our limited sphere.

"The words we speak are simply words; they have no value until others perceive them, take meaning from them, and act upon them, as we have said many times before. They are not *my* property, they are not *your* property; they are part of the universe. We ask you to protect them only to keep their purity and simplicity."

It was made clear at an early date that I was to write these teachings into a book.

Sometimes it was just Malcolm and I who sat in weekly session but a few close colleagues sat with us occasionally and one couple, Jean and Tom, later became regulars with Mo, who continued to help guide Malcolm's development and report her observations on our sittings. Malcolm's personal, and therefore emotional, state went through a turbulent period as his obsession with his psychic development increased far beyond the comprehension of his wife, who had also struggled in the earlier years of their relationship when he was prominent in the Trades Union Movement. Eventually, and perhaps inevitably, Malcolm and his wife separated and he quickly formed a close relationship with a friend he had known for some years. Although she had not previously been involved in spiritual matters, Pat also joined the sessions after a month or two and went on to be a comfort and great support to Malcolm in his work.

The evening sittings took place weekly at my home in the room set aside for healing and other spiritual work. Natural light or a table lamp lighted the room and a small table was set out with a candle and crystal on a white cloth. Malcolm sat in an oak carver chair and I was seated to his left with my pen and writing pad. Mo always placed herself centrally in order to observe while Pat sat to Malcolm's right and Jean and Tom between them, forming a small circle. After relaxing and sitting in silence for a while, Malcolm's breathing would deepen as he began to enter the first stage of trance. This might last for around 5 minutes, during which time he would be aware of ascending, or being drawn towards, a place of immense beauty and love. Completion of this stage was signalled by his body moving forward onto the edge of the chair and then a sudden jolt as the energy entered his form, causing his hands to fly apart and press against the inside of the chair arms. The information that his muscle power was enormous was very evident. This is how Zed explained the trance:

"Could I enlarge tonight on how we achieve between us the high levels of trance we need in order to communicate? Malcolm goes from a semi-trance to a fairly high level. This can be seen with his ability to contact Matthew but he is not able to go any higher than that unless in full trance. Imagine a pathway and you come to a fork: one path leads to a semi-trance state, but that path is limited in its distance and at the end of it is Matthew. If you choose the other, the trance pathway, you can also reach the level of

Matthew but you can go beyond, but only with the combined energies of the two of you.

"Just now, we showed you clearly how this was done. You observed Malcolm entering a trance state, you observed him reacting to the level of Matthew; that was the point where he sat on the edge of the chair. Then we did another thing this evening which we do many times to illustrate how we go higher: Malcolm held his hand to yours and the energies combined to reach that final level: if you like, it is like the key, it can only be turned by two, for reasons we have given before. That then opens you to the next level, and the level above if we should call upon it. This may seem a complicated procedure but if you think about it you can see the wisdom of combining energies to reach teachings of this high level.

"His arms flying apart; this is energy release when he hands over to us, like a combination surge, controlling exit and entry. It is the same energy but the force of many people coming together. Contained within the body the muscles and nerves react very strongly to the surge of energy and this needs tremendous control. His heart rate now is not as pronounced as it was before because he is more used to dealing with the combination of energies. You will have noticed the less dramatic ending of the trance now, and shorter; that comes with practice. The shivering he experiences (afterwards) is his body adapting to less energy and returning to normality. That 'hand-to-hand' exercise produces both stability and strength. So you see, the trance is very much the combined effort of the three of us."

Zed had previously commented on the changes taking place in Malcolm's body by telling us that "Physical force is needed because Malcolm has to operate in a certain way, but in terms of spiritual control it is like an elephant trying to control a fly: it needs fine tuning at our level." These physical changes included adjustments in Malcolm's throat that worried him to the extent that he sought medical advice. No ailment was found and the throat settled after a while.

Malcolm also discovered that his chest had expanded by several inches and he was able to breathe more deeply than before.

Always a great lover of his food, it took Malcolm a long while to come to terms with the reduction in his consumption of meat and alcohol that are hindrances to spiritual achievement, especially for a medium seeking to reach these levels. On one occasion there was an amusing but salutary incident when he insisted on buying a meat and potato pie for lunch despite being reminded that it was 'trance night'. His subsequent efforts to enter the trance state were laboured and accompanied by a series of loud rumblings and other indications of digestive disturbances. When Zed was finally able to come through he spoke with uncharacteristic sternness and said, "Never again must Malcolm eat meat before I come!"

From my perspective however, I knew that the form that sat in the chair and the voice that spoke were Malcolm's and yet, strange as it may seem, I ceased to identify with him as soon as Zed came through because as far as I was concerned, I was with another person. Mo once remarked that watching Zed and I together was like watching two lovers, although many years would pass before I understood the significance of this. But back then, the energy in the room changed with Zed's loving presence and we all felt privileged and humbled to be there.

As Malcolm was helped to 'step down' at the end of a session he often reported seeing us all as figures descending a great staircase, an indication that we had all occupied the same space and been equal participants in the experience. The effort left him utterly drained and parched until he finally became more practised. We would then move to another room and have a cup of tea while I read my account of what had transpired and added any comments or corrections from the others except Malcolm who, of course, had been totally unaware of what had been said.

During the summer of 1989 I was contacted by a researcher for Stephen Rose, a BBC television producer who was making a programme on healing for a series called 'Your Life In Their Hands'. I had previously been approached by another TV company but for some reason it had not felt right to proceed with them. What I came to realise over the years was the rather obvious fact that the integrity of almost any programme has to take second place to its public appeal factor. This is because programme-making costs money and funds must be bid for and considered on the basis of possible audience figures and subsequent distribution sales. Therefore the unfortunate fact that sensationalism equals good viewing figures accounts for much of the past coverage of peculiar practitioners and, to be honest, no doubt brought dynamic healing to Stephen's attention. This time however, I was happy to explore the possibility of cooperating in an established and well-respected series to hopefully help show a fascinating and yet at the same time a more sensible image of spiritual healing.

I felt the idea for this programme was part of Stephen's own spiritual quest and as such it perhaps stood a better chance of a balanced result. I also struck an immediate rapport with the assistant producer, another Jane, who later developed her own healing ability and remains a friend to this day. After months of various visits and meetings it was decided that the production team would film at my home over a 5-day period in September. The message that doors of public acceptance would be opened was beginning to ring true.

I went into a state of anxiety as the filming date approached, not from a lack of trust in any healing demonstration but from my confusion over what to wear since my wardrobe, like my income, had taken a definite downturn since my days of office suits. Finally I purchased an outfit that I thought was reasonably smart, only to discover when filming began that the producer required a change of clothing for each change of client. I almost began to envy the NFSH healers in their white hospital coats!

My healing room was too small to accommodate the team of producer, assistant producer, camera woman, assistant camera woman, sound recordist, the client and me, especially if any spontaneous movement were to happen. We therefore piled the furniture into the hallway and transferred operations to the living room.

In addition to several known clients, I was asked to find people who had not received healing before and who did not object to being filmed. As testament to the invisible stage-management that was undoubtedly going on behind the scenes, two ideal candidates came forward and responded to the healing with individually spontaneous movements, followed by articulate descriptions of their experience. One was a delightful elderly gentleman whose arthritis had severely restricted his arm and shoulder movements. As he stood with closed eyes in front of the camera, his right arm slowly moved out from his side and up above shoulder height for the first time in a number of years. I asked him if he was aware of his arm being raised and he opened his eyes, took a look, and said with some surprise, 'Well, so it is!'

Perhaps the more media-worthy of the new subjects was a tall butcher who was shown limping into the house with a chronic back condition and then performing a range of movements including shaking and back-bends that would clearly be impossible under normal circumstances. In fact, I was later told that a good deal of footage was edited out because Stephen felt the general public would simply not have believed it. The butcher – aptly named Colin Heal - was finally filmed walking away from the house with a smile on his face and minus the limp. I have a photograph of Colin taken a week or so later in dynamic healing, standing on his head against the wall of my room with the scars of an old spinal operation visible on his back.

Like many others, Colin was subsequently able to put himself into the 'healing mode' and self-correct when the need arose. He also developed the ability to heal others. Another amusing incident concerning Colin was when he brought his wife to me for healing and we couldn't find him when her session ended. Eventually we discovered him standing in the furthest corner of the garden where he said he had gone to 'get out of range' because he had been performing spontaneous dynamic healing movements in the living room. I have another set of photographs, taken later, of Colin in action being observed by a visiting Russian healer, Barbara Ivanova, who is sitting with her legs drawn up on her chair, trying to keep out of his way. She watched closely as Colin's body spontaneously contorted and stretched across the room, often using the furniture and walls in very precise ways to achieve certain positions. Barbara described the experience to a large audience at a public meeting organised by Dan Benor later that week, telling them, 'You have got to see it - I have never seen anything like this before.' No wonder then that my own presentation in the same town a week or two later was a complete sell-out.

It would be a further 18 months before the television programme was aired while Stephen followed up reports of other kinds of healing at home and in America. By the time it was shown the situation with the Zed group would be totally changed.

The need for meditation was emphasised time and again as the Zed sessions progressed and the Teachings began to reach a wider audience. Here is one passage:

"Looking to the future, simplicity and awareness of meditation in what you teach will play an increasing role in people's lives, for it is the key centre of your teaching. What we intend to do in the coming months, now that we have established our broad teachings, is to help you toward bringing mankind a step nearer to spiritual realisation. For we see a situation in the future where your teachings will be widely read and the lectures you give will form the basis of a new movement in which people will seek the answers within themselves and break from the complexities of the material world. This is why continual reference is made to the need for meditation. And here is the big one: *that the time will come when man can seek within himself the power to heal his own ailments and have complete unity with himself in a spiritual sense, thus fulfilling the objective of his presence on earth.* All the information you have at your disposal at the moment can set you on this path.

"Have courage, for it will not be easy. As a warning I will tell you this, that greedy people who see this as a challenge to the religions they have taught will seek to undermine you, for they have earned their wealth through complicating their religions to the point where the poor seeker can only seek salvation in either health or religion through complicated procedures involving more intelligent beings on this planet when in reality, what you will now be proposing is that they have all the answers they need within themselves at no cost to themselves or anyone else, but discipline, good living and good thinking. It's so simple!"

Malcolm was asked by Zed to formulate a course on meditation, which he did with the aid of Matthew's guidance and one of my sister Pamela's books on the ancient Indian Vipassana technique and Buddhist Mindful Approach that teaches the overcoming of the mind in the quest for freedom. I was asked to attend the initial courses to provide some background and thus we were both beginning to take the Teachings out to others, albeit on a modest basis.

Meditation workshops would also provide Malcolm with some much-needed income because he had not worked since giving up the retail enterprise he had shared with his wife, and he and Pat were living a hand-to-mouth existence. However, this counsel was given again, "But let them not use that knowledge for other than was intended, for throughout history wise teachings have been brought only to be corrupted and complicated in order that individuals can gain wealth and ego by misinterpreting them. And in your world today many individuals profit from complicating meditation and showing the only way to higher awareness is through paying a fee. We are offering you all the opportunity of washing the decks of misunderstanding and returning to the basic truth and simplicity of it all. A realistic fee is appropriate for you to live but seek not to grow rich from the teachings for this would be wrong."

One day while Malcolm and I were discussing possibilities for our courses, I visualised a space rocket with three stages: the first stage that lifted the rocket from the ground was dynamic healing. This then dropped away. The second stage that put the rocket on course was that of meditation. This then dropped away. And the third stage of the rocket went on alone. This was the individual's inner pathway. Shortly afterwards these words were received on the subject of teaching:

"We have our spiritual objectives but in seeking them we should also be ambassadors for the huge amount of love we have within, and when that love manifests, and the wisdom, others will understand. And this lines up with your rocket, Jane, for if we fill their hearts with love and understanding, then they will listen, but if we present our teachings in a cold analytical way, they are seen as just words, and then we run the risk of the means justifying the ends. So we see the teachings as paramount in our lives but we must also see them clearly illustrated and sitting on a pedestal of love, for then the seeker can take them to his heart. Therefore we have to develop in universal knowledge but also in love and compassion. We'd all like to think that our teachings were taught by gentle people."

The following 4 photographs are by John Stubbs
Camera 35mm with 50mm lens on tripod.
Film 400 asa in natural daylight. Speed 1/15th and 1/8th sec.
Straight prints.

A dynamic healing session begins

Spontaneous movement and brightness increase.

Strange brightness engulfs the client which we were later told was a kind of reaction between natural light and the healing energy field.

The weird light effects on the body and surrounding area
were not visible to the eye during the healing.

Chapter 7.

The idea of creating some kind of physical centre for the work was now being discussed by the group, partly due to Tom and Jean's forthcoming retirement and the sale of their pharmacy and shop. Tom had become aware of spiritual healing many years previously as a consequence of his daughter's death and his subsequent introduction to healing through the Atlantean Society. Even though healing could not prevent his daughter from dying, Tom recognised its value and took it into his life, but the loss of their child was a factor in the failure of Tom's marriage. Jean's first marriage had also ended in divorce and her meeting with Tom produced a certain 'chemistry', which was quite appropriate for a pharmacist! Throughout her childhood Jean had felt a sense of loss for a sister that had never, in fact, existed. So real did this sister seem that Jean even drew a picture of her – a girl of about ten with dark hair parted in the centre and braided into two plaits. Many years later she saw a photograph of Tom's daughter – and there was her sister! The likeness between the two images is uncanny.

It became apparent that each person in the group had their own ideas and agenda for having a centre: Jean and Tom to use their capital to pursue their healing ideals, Pat and Malcolm to have a home and income because by this time they had moved in with me, and Mo to be part of the group and its work. I had mixed feelings at the thought of selling the house that was so much more than my home but the idea of us all working and teaching under one roof had its attractions and I told myself that if this is what God wanted me to do, then I would do it. What I did not fully take on board was the rather obvious fact that although I was happy to work alongside others, I had a real struggle with being a team player.

From my childhood, through marriage, parenthood and other experiences up to that point I had learned to be independent and not to rely on other people. Perhaps I even mistrusted others. Conditioning also dictated that you 'got on with it' and didn't moan or discuss your feelings and although I knew from my counselling training that these were dangerous traits, I had not fully addressed them within myself. That space of safety that protected me as a child was hardening into a shell and I think I rather liked it. Independence meant that I could make my own choices without having to consult others, unless I wanted to. Independence meant that I could walk away from people and the choices they made, if I wanted to. Independence meant that I could manage my own time and resources. So why would I wish to change? After all, whilst independence has its selfish side, it had also served me well in allowing me to be single-minded in my spiritual pursuits. The thought of giving this up was not easy.

Zed had this to say on the subject of a centre:

"May we suggest to you all that a spiritual understanding is necessary before you can hope to go forward in a practical way? All of you have reached different levels of spiritual awareness and all of you have reached different levels of knowledge and expertise. You all tend therefore to look at yourselves from the level you have reached and differently perhaps at others who have not your knowledge and understanding and are unable to grasp the meaning of what you say. It is important therefore, to grow closer together in love of each other, to deepen the understanding and share the knowledge between you, for if you choose the pathway of unity, you must share a bond of understanding to build on.

"Some of you have many years of experience, others are just starting. The importance of each one of you is equal. This is no different from the spirit world, as we have indicated before. Seniority does not exist in terms of levels, only of understanding, so let us all be tolerant of each other.

Then armed with that knowledge, will you not be in a better position to choose the path to follow? Could we suggest that an evening or two could be set aside to share experiences and knowledge with each other? It is not our intention to point you in any direction but merely to harmonise you so you can develop your own conclusions. Apologies for our terminology again but we hope you have the broad principles."

We adopted the evenings of discussion but any resulting unity was questionable, for essentially we hear what we want to hear.

"Always there is choice. People ask why we don't arrange events the way we would wish but that would be wrong. We can create the doors of choice but it is up to you whether you walk through them."

Crystals were also used to advantage in my healing work, always using small pieces of rose quartz that would fit within the palm of a hand and many were attuned and given out over the years with directions to hold the stone gently, be still, and ask for healing. They were greatly valued by those who received them. The following is the story of one recipient, as written at the time.

'5th May 1990. This was Spencer's third visit, the first two having been about three weeks ago. It started when a young woman who had been to see me for healing rang and asked if I would see her cousin who was 17 years old and who'd had leukaemia since the age of ten. He lived some 200 miles away but would be coming to stay with his aunt for a few days, provided he was well enough.

Spencer's condition was obviously fragile but I was utterly charmed by this delightful young man with his warm wide smile and air of calm. Not very tall and extremely thin except for his cheeks (the effect of long term steroids), his breathing was shallow and laboured as he explained that his lungs were 'packing up' but his medication had to be reduced because it was now weakening his spine. He tried to keep his lifestyle as normal as possible but this was difficult as even gentle walking tired him greatly.

Spencer and his family felt he was having the best attention the medical world could offer and they complied with all the advice and treatments and tests. In addition, however, they scanned a wider horizon and made use of a dietary plan that seemed to make sense, plus weekly visits to a local spiritual healer and monthly visits to another one about 40 miles away. Spencer felt the benefit from both these healers and perhaps thought that seeing me whilst on holiday would maintain the continuity.

After talking for a while in my healing room we began the first session as I explained that he may experience various sensations or even involuntary body movements without direction or touch from me. He quickly slipped into a relaxed inner space and his head and neck began gyrating powerfully followed by marked movements in his trunk from a standing position. Spencer was fascinated.

We worked for over an hour, after which his breathing had deepened and he said he felt generally better and stronger. We had only 2 days before he returned home so I suggested I would ask Malcolm to attune a rose-quartz crystal for him to help him align to the energy and continue the self-healing.

I offered Spencer a little top-up when he came to collect the crystal and, watched by his mother, the healing movements became stronger and more pronounced. As he sat on a stool, his body leaned right back, his legs straightened off the floor and his arms described large circles. Then from a prone position on the treatment couch his arms became even more active as he described the sensations within and the changing colours he could see within his closed eyes. His left arm arched above his chest, the fingertips appeared to place themselves precisely into positions, and Spencer reported that he could feel cold energy coming out of them and flowing into his lungs. By this time his mother was in tears but we were all smiling broadly and aware of the energy of love filling the room.

The 'little top-up' lasted an hour and a half and at the end of it Spencer was almost shining. I gave him instructions on healing himself and a fortnight later had a lovely letter to say he was carrying on the good work and feeling better than for ages, although he couldn't wait to come back for another session.

So today he came. The steroids were now reduced by half and his breathing, and therefore activity, had been much improved until the past two days when it had become more difficult. His mother and aunt went off to the beach, saying Spencer's father would be back to wait for him.

Spencer told me that the crystal hadn't left his side since he received it and showed me that it was in his pocket now. We began the session with him sitting, then standing to allow more 'leverage' for the movements, and then he lay on the couch. By this stage the inward vision of colours was growing and Spencer's breathing was already smoother. While this was going on we talked about the meaning of illness and he said that when he had a good day he could think he was learning from it but it was much harder when he had a bad day and then he would think he was being punished for something. He told me he often thought there must be a purpose to life but he hadn't worked out what it is, although he liked to listen to other people's ideas.

We shared together our sensations and inner seeing as I worked slowly through his energy. When my hands moved over his solar plexus, his diaphragm and chest rose and fell dramatically and once again, with the crystal in his right palm, Spencer's fingers went to specific points on his chest and particularly the base of his right lung, which he said felt like an area of stretching and clearing out. Then after some time his arms started to stretch outwards at right angles to his body, opening the rib cage as he breathed deeply, then pulling upwards above his head as though he were being stretched on the rack. All this time we continued our dialogue. When I reached his head, Spencer experienced an even greater intensity of white, pink and gold light and then described thousands of brilliantly coloured 'dots' that formed a tunnel through which he passed into a vast space filled with love and energy.

Still in a prone position, Spencer's arms and hands began to move in new patterns, first from one side to the other, which he said he knew were balancing his energy. Then came what appeared to be positive and very beautiful T'ai Chi movements, slow to begin with but building into 'harder' configurations. At one stage his thumbs and index fingers formed a triangle above his head that was then moved down to rest with the point at his brow. The triangle then narrowed and he began to rub his eyes, mainly with the side of his thumbs and at times quite hard. He said this felt good and thought it was healing his eyes, which had dark circles as though he had painted the lids with charcoal and then rubbed them with his knuckles. Spencer was thrilled with the movements, which were all outside his conscious control, and he said, "I feel so *strong* - I haven't felt this strong for years and years!" He told me he had been fascinated by martial arts since he was small but had been unable to practice any because of his condition.

Then with his legs straight along the couch, he suddenly sat up and after a pause brought his knees up and put his head down. He was quiet for a few moments and then said, "That was the unborn child."

Deftly, he then sat up, put his legs apart and straddled the couch. "It wants me to undo my belt" he said, and unfastened his wide leather belt and untucked his long sweatshirt. The arm movements began again and now he was a Samurai warrior wielding a great two-handed sword in complex patterns, complete with sounds and facial movements. It was truly amazing and I stood back and watched in awe.

I am well aware that those who experience such powerful dynamic healing cannot adequately describe them to their family afterwards because they are truly out of the norm. For Spencer's sake I asked him if he would like me to fetch his dad from where he was waiting in the other room and with obvious surprise he replied that he'd just had the same thought.

Spencer's father could hardly believe his eyes when he came in and saw his son breathing strongly and performing movements that had been simply unthinkable for so long. And yet more was to come.

"It wants me to get off the couch" Spencer said and swung himself around and onto the floor. He fastened his belt again and somehow looked the part with his blue and gold sweatshirt hanging loose outside his pale cotton trousers, standing now in a martial arts stance with elbows bent and trunk at right angles to his parted legs. Now came a phase of powerful arm and body movements, again with shouts and facial expressions, some slow, some extremely fast and complex and ending with a rapid clenched fist thrust from which we could feel the energy.

Other patterns of movement were performed laying on the floor or sitting as 'it' directed and by now Spencer could see his arms and legs with his eyes closed, not as with normal vision but as if his limbs were made of light. He also said that his brain told him he was in my healing room but he actually felt as if he were in a huge space where on his right hand side (the window side) he was in brilliant gold light and on his left (where I stood) the light was shining pink, and it was all very beautiful.

The feeling in the room was indescribable and all three of us were in a state of wonderment. What happened next came as a further total surprise, for another voice entered the proceedings!

Speaking through an amazed Spencer who was perfectly aware and awake, the voice spoke effortlessly in a rather clipped style and with less movement of the lips like an Oriental, but still sounding like Spencer. Can you imagine the effect this had on the teenager, hearing words coming out of his own mouth without his intention and voicing words he had not thought of?

The Voice announced itself with a Chinese-sounding name, something like 'Chow-Li', and quickly established that it was helping Spencer. It had a great sense of humour. At some point in the proceedings it told Spencer to take tissues from his pocket and he then began to cough up quantities of phlegm. When this was over, his hand rolled the tissues up like a magician performing a trick and Spencer said he was sure they were going to disappear. At this remark the Voice joined in and said, 'Ah yes! I am the Magic Man – the Magic Man within you!"

This turn of events set my mind in a whirl; after all, I was not used to this kind of 'jokey' behaviour in my room and I had always tried to ensure that only energies of the highest spiritual level were sought. I struggled for a while and finally decided to return to *trust*: after all, I sensed that everything felt right and in my 20 years of healing I could not recall a single adverse outcome. Still, I had never witnessed anything like this.

As if reading my thoughts the Voice said, "It is good to laugh, yes! It is right to have fun, not to be always full of gloom!" It then went on with guidance for the teenage Spencer that was of such a personal nature that it almost took my breath away. The movements continued all the while until finally Spencer reported that it had told him he could put his shoes on now. The vigorous movements had lasted for over an hour: heavy going for a fit person but completely amazing for Spencer, who was now glowing with strength and laughing with delight.

Spencer pointed the fingers of his right hand at his father who was sitting opposite and the Voice said, "You have trouble in your back. When you have pain, lay on the bed and

Spencer will put his hands on you and the pain will ease." Then he turned to me and asked, "This work you do, does it tire you?" "Well, I have to re-charge my energy." I replied. "Quite so," said the Voice. "Spencer must also build his energies. He may ease pain but not cure yet. One day he will also be a healer and he will have fame and fortune – not that fortune is important but, ah, it may make life easier!" In the strange three-way conversation of two people and three voices, advice came on health and family matters and the Voice also said that Spencer's brother would bring him to see me next time – a prediction that surprised both him and his father.

Spencer's father finally remarked that they had better go down to the town to find his wife and her sister, as it was now lunchtime. Spencer said, "I'm hungry" and the Voice immediately responded, "Yes, let us go and buy food!" We wondered how they would be able to relate the morning's events and the Voice chipped in with, "You will not hear me when you leave the energies of this room – we do not want people to think you are a p**t!" We all laughed. "Yes" it went on, "I must use Spencer's language, otherwise how would he understand me?"

I have been told, and I believe without doubt, that my healing room is protected against unwelcome or inappropriate intrusions of any kind and therefore what Spencer experienced that day was for good reason. As may be imagined, it gave him much food for thought and set him even more firmly on a pathway of spiritual exploration that included coming to workshops on healing and meditation where his wisdom and good humour shone like a beacon amongst the older participants. Some months later he told me, "I am not afraid to die."

So who or what was the voice that spoke through him and where did it come from? My own impression is that it was not from some outside source but was either an aspect of

Spencer's inner personality from a previous lifetime or perhaps a closely connected entity from that time. If this were so then it was not the first time that a previous incarnation had come to the fore during a healing session, as with my friend Valerie, although not as dramatically as this, I have to say. In either case, what happened was by agreement with Spencer's higher self within the healing energies of the room so I was content.

Many years ago I had the privilege of working with an elderly lady whose daughter brought her for healing over a period of a year or so. This lady, whom I shall call Ellen, was small and timid like a little bird, and suffered from an arthritic condition that restricted her mobility. She had been a professional pianist in the past, playing mainly at tea dances and the like, and the stiffness in her joints was now affecting her ability to play even for her own pleasure.

Ellen responded quickly and dynamically to the healing and performed wonderfully elegant exercises that resembled those of a ballet dancer limbering up. One of these movements was to sit down (or as she would say, 'be sat down') on the floor with her legs crossed and then to take hold of an ankle and lift her leg straight up in the air with no apparent effort: easy enough for a lithe dancer perhaps, but amazing for an arthritic lady of advanced age. We also used the sessions to gently explore her lack of confidence and I like to think this too made a difference to her general wellbeing. Then one day she came and told me about something that had happened that week whilst she was sitting quietly at the piano in her daughter's house, playing an old dance tune. Without warning, everything changed and powerful and beautiful music flowed out, the like of which she had never heard. Her daughter hurried into the room as the music ended, clearly puzzled. "Was that you?" she asked her mother. Ellen too was confused, for how do you explain that your hands produced something so beautiful but so alien entirely on their own? To me, this was yet another dynamic demonstration by the higher self of the love and beauty that lies within each of us.

The subject of the environment was not forgotten and many groups as well as our own used their meetings for healing the planet. Zed linked this to the teachings on meditation.

"We have talked of the individual and the need for meditation. We have talked of the need to help the human race be more aware of what they do to the planet. By making them more aware of their spiritual pathway they become more aware of what they do to the planet. The two are not opposed but complementary, for what spiritually aware person could possibly hurt this beautiful planet and all the creatures that live on it?

"The process of learning is speeding up and man is becoming more aware. The time period, however, is short, and always remember that the choice is yours: there will be no divine intervention to stop you ruining this beautiful planet, as many would have you believe. Only by your increased awareness can it be stopped, for if divine intervention were the answer, then there would be no point in you being here. Always there is choice."

Although we were not robbed of our choice, we were fortunate to receive guidance on a more personal level when it was appropriate to our spiritual understanding and development. The following is one example: "I have told you the important roles you all have to play in the future. We can only suggest but it needs you to act. And as your energies grow, as you become aware of what you call the dynamic energy and strength, the more it will grow in all of you. These are exciting times but as your influence grows so also will your critics, for there will always be those who seek to undermine you: that is part of your test. Return always to the words. Keep the words as pure and simple as you can: simple, but profound. What you are about to start is new and exciting because it embodies historic interest with modern interpretations and a greater energy than man has seen before. You are the forerunners and those that follow you will grow even stronger."

Another essential piece of advice was this: "Practise patience and be tolerant of those among you who have not the awareness: love them all and help them towards the pathway. Do so as far as possible with no ego, for it has no purpose; it is an earthbound emotion and one that can turn your head with great ease."

We had asked whether the communicators also worked with other groups and were told, "Mankind's desire is to ruin the planet and our desire is that he should not. To that end we have helped this and other groups. But the teachings are with you only."

The theme was continued at the next sitting:

"Consider the source of our thought: it is like that of a mountain stream. High up the water is little and pure: such are our teachings. That is why, Jane, we have just one stream, for more would run the risk of pollution. So when our thoughts reach you they are pure, and from there they go further and the stream becomes a river, and as the river runs over the stones of interpretation so the message becomes obscure. So you see the wisdom of us speaking straight to you."

The responsibility of recording and sharing the teachings did not sit lightly with me. The title 'ambassador' was added to that of 'scribe' and yet the effort of seeing clients, organising workshops and groups for Malcolm as well as myself, transcribing sessions and dealing with daily housekeeping matters with two extra people in my home resulted in bouts of exhaustion. Clearly, I needed to learn to apply balance to my own life and yet at the time I felt driven by a sense of urgency. Unfortunately, it was also in my nature to try and control everything instead of delegating, so in that respect I was the architect of my own ills. At such times I was treated very lovingly during the sessions and sometimes given healing by Zed, when he would lean forward and place his hands around my head. This is what I wrote after one such occasion: 'I looked at him and began to cry, feeling such a painful sense of longing. And for the first time Zed silently cried too: a large tear welling from each closed eye and running down Malcolm's cheeks.'

There was another instance some time previously, when Zed was much firmer in reminding me that I had been told that Malcolm was my reservoir so why was I not making use of this? It was suggested that Malcolm would attune to me each day at 7.30 a.m. to give me a 'boost' of energy. After some weeks of this, I looked in the mirror after my lone sitting one morning and saw a one-eyed monster staring back at me: a blood vessel had broken in my left eye. Malcolm was sheepish when he saw me later and admitted that he'd decided to give the attunement a miss that day. My bloodshot eye was clearly meant as a lesson for him.

But on the subject of suffering and dynamic healing, the following words from Zed in the April of that year formed one of the greatest influences on my life:

"Consider the stream that we spoke of before. As it flows down we see it as the stream of life, and as it flows further down so it grows in magnitude and speed, and from the birth as a small stream to the adult as a river, this now river of life has on its left bank many who walk in the direction of the current, for the left bank is the bank of *ego*. Those who understand less carry on walking towards the mouth of the river but if they were to look right they would see the bridges of spiritual awareness and cross to the bank of *love*. But on that side they would be away from the view of all those that surround them, for here on the left bank of ego many follow them: they have great power, great prestige, great riches, and people shout their names and call them 'great ones'. But the truly great one is she that walks to the right bank where no riches, no materialism, no recognition except that of shared love exists. The four of you will stand at the entrance to that bridge and explain to those that need to cross that it's not an easy pathway for it is contrary to all they have learned, but it is not a long bridge either.

"Can you see similarities, all of you, in what we say, with the life around you? The problem is, you see, that until they reach the right bank they are obscured from their spiritual progress."

I asked, what will motivate them to want to cross? Zed replied, "Those that lead - very little! But those who seek will become disillusioned with what they see, for the leaders are so bound up with their ego that they don't even recognise that a bridge exists: they question the whole concept of spiritual awareness. But those who seek will soon discover the hollowness of the reasoning of these ego-hunters and will look for a deeper meaning in their lives. That is where your dynamic healing is so important Jane, for they are motivated initially by a cure to their illnesses, but soon they learn that this was nothing, merely a lesson in direction to their real awareness, and in learning from their illness they see the true pathway *over the bridge*. So now you see the need, why it is so important that your teaching and demonstrations in dynamic healing should reach as many as possible.

"You both are looking forward to a new challenge and helped by Pat and Maureen (Mo) you can see the magnitude of your task. You have a rare gift, old friend, and it was no accident that you chose to bring it, for unlike many believe, they are gifts to yourself that you bring with you - necessary tools in experience and teaching in life."

It was difficult not to become excited by the information that was coming through the sittings and I would often engage in long debates over the meaning of some issue or another, in spite of Zed warning us, "You do not need high intellect to understand the secrets of the universe when you have within you a complete encyclopaedia of its contents." I well recall a meeting when Tom, Malcolm and I in particular were indulging our minds over some point while Jean, Pat and Mo remained almost silent. Mo said that as she sat alone afterwards, feeling depressed because she had not understood a word of the discussion, she slipped into a meditation and was instantly aware of the meaning of the subject with complete clarity. A prime example that knowledge is one thing and awareness is another!

Mo was now working with other groups and introducing them to the Teachings under the guidance of Matthew. Although such spiritual pursuits were new to Pat, she was disciplined with her meditation practice and became increasingly intuitive. For me, any psychic 'pictures' were very rare and I was told this was because I had chosen to direct all my energy through my hands. However, when a vision arrived it was always vivid and to the point.

On one occasion, Zed asked me to tell him about a particular experience I'd had some years previously when I had booked a session with a lady who worked with what she called a creative visualisation technique. I lay comfortable and warm on cushions on the floor of her living room for an hour while she tried her best to guide me to visualise images but none came: the screen was blank. Then as we finally gave up and I was about to move, I suddenly found myself sitting in my old infants school classroom, the only pupil amid the rows of double desks with flip-up seats. In front of me on a dais was a blackboard with, I think, some simple sum in white chalk, and to one side of it was a teacher in a black gown and mortarboard. I rose from my little desk and moved sideways into the narrow gangway. Then as I approached the teacher I was suddenly aware that it had no face, there was just a hole, and with that realisation I then became the teacher standing on the dais, looking out over the classroom.

Zed asked me, "And how did you interpret that dream?" I answered that I thought it meant that I have come to this life to both learn and teach. Zed replied, "But do you not see that the teacher represented your higher self? How many people were left in the class?" None, I said. "So that was your body merging with your higher self." I told him that I hadn't realised that and he said, "You see the importance of meditation." Yes. He said, "It's a pity you didn't finish the dream, for the teacher walked out of the classroom and the world listened."

We were also given some interesting information about dreams, which fall into two categories. In the first category, the subconscious part of the mind is active, which is necessary for our health and can be observed by the sleeper's rapid eye movements even though such dreams are seldom fully remembered on waking. The second category happens only rarely, if at all, and this is when a state of no-mind occurs during sleep and there is no barrier to the higher self. Contrary to some beliefs, this kind of sleep state cannot be induced, but why bother anyway when it can happen in meditation? My experience is that the 'higher self dream' is totally different from the usual kind of dream in that it is vivid and can be clearly recalled in detail, sometimes for years afterwards, even if it didn't seem to make sense at the time. My higher self dreams have almost invariably used images of various forms of transport, from a baby carriage to a double-decker bus: I think my higher self must have a good sense of humour.

One example was a vivid and detailed dream I had at a particularly busy and stressful time: I was standing on the platform of the local railway station, waiting for the London train to take me to a meeting, when a young couple came up to me and asked me to look after their bags while they went and had a cup of tea in the station buffet. They dropped their baggage at my side and went off and my train arrived. Succinct! Needless to say, I had been allowing myself to be repeatedly diverted from my spiritual objectives by other people's demands of me.

By August 1990 Tom and Jean were able to join the weekly sessions and were commended on their trust because until then they had only seen transcripts of the meetings. Plans for their retirement and setting up a spiritual centre continued, the first synopsis of the Teachings book was sent to a publisher, and Saddam Hussein invaded Kuwait under the guise of a holy war. This is what Zed had to say on the latter subject,

"See the foolishness of religious teachings and how they are being used in the world today, for no religion can justify the killing of thousands. The Universal Love and God in us all is the same, whether they be American, European, or Arab: the God of Love runs through you all. Yet one half is motivated by material ambition in one direction and one half by material ambition in another, and you seek to blame God for it. This religious corruption has got to stop! It matters not how you perceive God but only that you understand God for what He is." We set out with our groups to send thoughts of love and peace into the world.

Mo was experiencing little peace in her domestic life at this juncture. However, after years of anxiety at the prospect of taking on the emotional and financial burdens of being a single parent to her three children, she finally knew intuitively that this was the time to end an increasingly difficult marriage. Our sessions were a sanctuary of love and friendship for her during this turbulent period and Zed's words were full of comfort and understanding.

"We have turned your world upside-down, My Eyes, but that is why you came. But always, as we've said before, you have choice. Love you see as the very core of you, love of all you see around you, and yet those values are alien to those you walk with at present. We understand but we cannot help. You see, it's a misconception that we possess the right to do so at our levels. You chose the path of experience and you have the right of choice. We can only walk with you with love and understanding. We can hold you when you cry, we can help lift you up when you fall down, but each step you take must be yours, it must be so."

Spencer had not been well enough to visit for a while so we kept in touch by telephone. He told me he had been offered a heart/lung transplant and that whilst he was 'not bothered' about accepting, he felt he had to go ahead for the sake of his family. A donor eventually became available and Spencer had the transplant. He rallied bravely after the operation but then perhaps because of the ravages of the illness on his body over so many years, the organs failed and Spencer died. How his parents and family dealt with his loss is beyond imagination. I hesitate to apply the word 'special' to any individual, but Spencer was.

I went into my room and lit a candle when I heard the news. Suddenly I was filled with a kind of excitement and my face broke into an ear-to-ear grin. No doubt who was here! With great enthusiasm he told me, "It's great Jane – it's everything you said it was!"

Fumi in meditation

Spencer spent much of his time at home trying to capture the kind of images he saw in his mediations, often sending his mother back to the art shop for more colours but never quite managing to find what he wanted. In this painting he has expanded on a diagram I often used in my workshops which depicts his physical self (the small triangle) resting on the planet whilst his higher self experiences the universe.

Chapter 8

With hindsight I am not surprised that the first synopsis of the book came back from the publishers and it might be reasonable to ask why there had been so much encouragement for producing a book when the Teachings were still in progress. Perhaps the answer lay in my enthusiasm and lack of patience and yet I genuinely believed I was responding to a sense of urgency from the communicators. I don't know how I would have felt had I known then how many years would pass before the Teachings would finally appear in print. The following is an example of what we were being told at the time.

"How much better it would be in this so-called age of scientific enlightenment and technology, if Homo sapiens put his mind to the purpose for which he came instead of seeking the pathways of self-destruction. Each time we meet, the dire need for a change of direction of the society in which you live must become obvious to you. If you search our teachings of a few months back, and if you see them recently, you can see now the wisdom of what we say and how man uses religion in pursuance of political gain. Such is going on in the world right now. We have no wish to negate the world's karma, and entities at our level will not predict the future, but when we give you lessons and teachings, the wise mind can interpret the reasons for such teachings and use them for world events as they occur, thus seeing the true spiritual pathway to take. So if the teachings were available to all those at the moment who lead their peoples in religious and pseudo-religious dogma, would not wise minds amongst them see clearly what their leaders were at? They would not, would they, be able to develop and drill hatred against their fellow man for gain? Such has been the case throughout man's history because of the nature of the mind, the appeal of material gain, the insatiable need for sensation. If we stooped to such measures there is little doubt that we would win all the support we need, but what useful purpose would that serve, to negate the choice of mankind?   We must hope, mustn't we, that enlightened ones amongst you will see the wisdom of the words you have written, Jane, and help secure the distribution of our work which is so desperately needed. Why, you ask, do you not open the doors to such proposals? (Choice?) Right. Such would be direct interference would it not?

"Imagine a lonely man walking along a pathway; you wish to construct another path leading away from the one he is walking, a pathway that leads directly to our bridge over the river. Such pathways have to be correctly made; they must be firm, with a brick construction. We supply you with those bricks - bricks of words - and you lay them in the direction the man can walk. And as you walk along that new pathway, we will provide new bricks for you so you will get closer to your goal. But it's true that the more that follow you, the faster the pathway will be built. When it is built, many will walk along it for they can see its destination clearly, but at the moment all we can offer is one away from the material pathway and there's only a few bricks to be seen."

I sent the synopsis to a literary agent but again it was returned. With hindsight this is not surprising as it was a very short and amateur affair.

Talks on the creation of a spiritual centre were continuing with the six members of the group and we were counselled to consider these words:

"So in pursuing your objective, see clearly your real value and at each step you take consider the implications of what you do and who you are, and consider the motivations that make you take them. Search yourselves for the motivating force within you and let love alone be your motivating force. How can you teach people what we have to

110

say if your internal emotions are in turmoil? When you have love you no longer have fear; it no longer plays a part in the pathway you walk. For as you learn the teachings, so you need to increase your own awareness to make good use of them. For when we said you were ambassadors of yourself, we meant that. And the teachings we bring are not only ours, but yours: we only bring them to the conscious mind but they are there already."

At the same time I was attempting to take the Teachings out through workshops, talks and written articles. It was not long before I received some wise guidance from Zed when I complained of being too tied up in detail.

"It is important to look at life objectively, rather than subjectively. Do you think it is possible you look at it subjectively sometimes? Perhaps that is an avenue of thought you could pursue, for it may show you the reality of your work. Maybe it is just a question of clarity of understanding, for if you thrust your energies towards a given goal, do you not create the inability within yourself to reach it? If you have clarity within you of the way to walk, then pressure is no longer there. Sometimes our activities become so diverse that we lose sight of where we are going and to overcome that we seek further diversities instead of consolidating the path we already walk. We wish to show the world what we have learned and we seek all avenues to do this, and in seeking those avenues they become an end in themselves and we forget our objective. For the avenues open to us are conditioned by others but we alone are responsible for our objectives.

"We stand in a room and in our hand we have the Teachings, and in front of us are a thousand doors we may walk through. We rush from one door to the other, opening them in an endeavour to show the Teachings to all. But sometimes we forget that all those doors lead into the same room on the other side and if we had opened just one of those doors and walked through with determination, taking those

Teachings with us, we would have had all the audience we needed on the other side."

One example of my tendency for rushing at things was when I was holding a weekend workshop for a group in London. As I launched into yet another aspect of the Teachings on the morning of the second day, the group groaned and protested, 'Don't tell us any more, we can't take it all in!' That was a great learning for me. Until then I had felt compelled to pass over as much information as possible in the shortest time possible and thereby had ignored the very essence of the careful manner in which Zed had been working with us. There were two important things I needed to take on board: 1) that time to digest is essential and 2) that knowledge is of little use without experience.

There is no doubt that one of the most popular aspects of my workshops was the group dynamic healing or, as I call it for short, the GDH, where everyone present was asked to stand or sit and relax and allow themselves to receive healing. Sessions would last from 15 to 50 minutes and groups ranged in number from just a few people to a hall of 80 or so. The aim of the GDH, as with all spiritual healing, was so much more than the alleviation or cure of illness for, as Zed taught us, suffering has only one purpose, and that is to raise awareness.

As previously indicated, I have seldom felt the need to touch a client during a session and am often a few feet or more away if they are in strong self-correcting movement so I found it quite acceptable that a roomful of people could respond without physical contact. I also knew that the energy available was greater than I could possibly imagine and my role was therefore to relax and help create a kind of healing environment and then simply trust the process. There were a few occasions in the early days when I was a little concerned if someone went down on their face like a felled tree, for example, but I learned from experience that the person is always quite relaxed and no harm is done, although obviously I take time afterwards to check on every individual.

Anything is possible in a GDH and I am privileged to have witnessed outcomes ranging across physical corrections, emotional releases, insights into causes, psychic connections and spiritual experiences. Once again I stress that any movements in dynamic healing are involuntary, as if the body is manipulating itself without conscious control. In fact, the mind could be said to stand to one side like an interested spectator or to feel itself occupying a different and beautiful space from which it often does not wish to return. The kind of descriptions that follow a session are: 'it pulled me down to the floor and I couldn't get up', 'it made me touch my toes, which I haven't been able to do for years', 'I know I was banging the floor but I couldn't stop it', and 'I was in a place of incredible light and peace.' I really have to mention that on several occasions I have seen someone fall over backward without any effort to save themselves and come to rest carefully positioned between two obstacles which, had they fallen an inch or so either way, could easily have caused an injury. One of these was in a school hall where an elderly lady landed with her head neatly placed between big heating pipes on one side and the base of a very large wooden blackboard on wheels on the other. When asked, she reported that she'd had a lovely experience, thank you.

There is often a not-unreasonable desire on the part of some participants to experience dynamic movement but I try to explain that some of the most powerful results of healing have come when the person has been quite still and nothing appeared to be happening. One such case concerned a young woman in her early twenties who remained motionless during a group healing on the first day of a weekend workshop. She was, however, emotionally upset after the session and just said, 'She didn't deserve to be taken away, she wasn't mad.' She made it clear that she did not want further discussion but later contacted me to tell her story. It seems that when she was a child, her grandmother who lived with the family, had been taken away and the girl had been told it was because the grandmother was mad. This event had grieved the child deeply. The girl grew up but did not biologically mature into the woman and medical investigations could find no cause. "I went home from the workshop, she told me, "and to put it crudely, the floodgates opened."

Another example of how emotional trauma can cause physical symptoms was when a lovely old gentleman came for healing on terrible eczema that covered his face with brilliant red blotches that medication had failed to alleviate, causing him great distress. After he had relaxed into the healing I asked him why he thought the eczema had started and without hesitation he replied that some time ago he'd had a motor accident. In fact, he'd had two accidents, neither of them serious, but he felt very guilty and had given up driving. Until the healing session he had not connected the accidents with the eczema but the condition had completely cleared by the time of his next visit.

Emotional traumas are important on every level for they lie like sodden blankets of energy within us, causing physical and mental disturbances that are hindrances to our earthly and spiritual progress until they are acknowledged. To be aware of a trauma and yet suppress or ignore it is to allow it to fester until sooner or later that energy will rise to the surface and emerge by way of behaviour or illness. We cannot escape the consequences of our experiences and so our best course of action is to deal with them and use them as signposts along the way. As the title of this book says, 'All the trials of life are meaningless unless we learn from them.'

Mo was encouraged to speak of her trauma and difficulty in coping with being alone and feeling lonely, to which Zed replied,

"This may not seem relevant at this stage, but true aloneness is real freedom. That does not mean being divorced from those around you, your children and loved ones, but when you are truly alone you see the true reality of your existence."

These words reminded me of a time when I was feeling low and sad after the death of my sister. I was sitting in meditation with Malcolm when Matthew came through and after a short discussion he asked me, "But you *chose* to be alone, didn't you?" and those words struck to my core with a truth I recognised. "Yes" I immediately replied without thinking, and from that day on I have seldom known anything but great contentment with my aloneness. Again, I can also see from this distance in time how my early childhood experiences had provided the ideal foundation for this state.

I had not always been on my own though, and a few years previously I'd had a relationship with a man whose daughter had died from a heart condition when she was little. One day while I was giving him healing on a back complaint, my arm was pushed away by some invisible force and I told him, "Someone's just pushed my arm away and said, 'That's *my* daddy!' "Oh yes, he replied calmly, "that's exactly what my little girl used to say if anyone came near us." We were both also aware that his daughter sometimes wriggled in between us on the sofa.

Even stranger perhaps were the visits from two of my old cats, a mother and daughter, who occasionally came to sit beside me for some years after their deaths. The older of these two had been with me since before Michael was born and took on the role of nanny, running to get me if the baby cried and deliberately letting him play with her tail. We were all upset when she died of old age but one night shortly afterwards when I was lying in the dark I felt her jump up onto the foot of the bed and make her way unsteadily up the covers toward me. The most striking thing was her weight, which was as physical as if she were actually there. Dear old friend – I was happy to know she was still around.

I have a particular fondness for cats and as with my first healing attempt, they have played a major role in my life. This is the story of another of them:

I had a call one day from a lady who asked, "Do you heal cats?" "Well, not usually, I replied, "but tell me the problem." She told me that her cat, a year-old ginger tabby by the name of Henry, had been struck by a car but the only injury he sustained was that the nerves to his tail had been severed. The vet advised amputation but the lady wished to explore alternatives before agreeing: hence the call. I went to her house and there was Henry, fit and handsome except for his tail, which he was dragging along the floor behind him like a piece of string. I sat him in an armchair and knelt down to give him healing, which he seemed to enjoy. After a while his owner (if cats have such a thing) came in and asked what I thought she should do about the amputation. I replied that it was not my place to advise on such matters but that if Henry were my cat I would ask the vet if it would be safe to delay the operation for a few days just to see if the healing had any effect. With that, Henry jumped down from the chair, stuck his tail out behind him and walked out of the door!

It transpired that this lady was a volunteer with a cats rescue organisation and so of course she sounded me out on the possibility of homing one of their many charges. I already had a cat, Wilfred Herbert, a confirmed outdoors dweller that my son had found sick and starving on a farm. However, two years previously I had been offered a little black kitten with white paws but had refused to take him because I felt it might upset Wilfred. Now I confessed to this lady that I had deeply regretted my decision when I heard that its owners had subsequently drowned this kitten. I told her that I was not actively looking for another cat but if they had a kitten that they really, really could not home elsewhere then she could give me a ring. Needless to say, it wasn't long before the call came and I went back to the house where Henry and his tail, by the way, were still attached and doing fine.

I waited in the front room and suddenly a tiny black kitten with white socks ran through the doorway and straight onto my lap and into my heart. With his big round eyes, white whiskers and white bib, I thought he was the most beautiful creature I had ever seen. I like to think it was love at first sight for both of us and for the next eighteen years Basil and I were virtually inseparable. Those readers who love their pets will know what I mean when I say that Basil was always there for me, ready with his warmth and affection regardless of anything that might be happening in the wider world, and in that respect he was a great support for me through troubled times. He would jump onto my lap at every opportunity and lie on his back in my arms like a baby or sprawl across me with his four legs in the air in a state of complete relaxation and trust. Basil often managed to sneak into the room when the meditation group met but I had to ban him from my private meditations due to his loud purring and the possibility of him jumping on me unexpectedly. He was gracious with neighbours and callers to the house but jealous of Wilfred and a positive virago to feline trespassers. Now, years after his passing, I occasionally feel him get up on my lap, and psychic visitors see him ambling around the house in his stately old way.

The Teachings of Zed explain in simple terms how everything on this planet is a manifestation of universal energy and interacts with everything else, be it animal, vegetable or mineral. They teach that only human beings have gained the capacity to exist beyond the earth levels of 1 and 2 at present but that other animal species may in time evolve to join them provided, we are warned, that we allow them to survive. They go on,

"The time has come in your evolution to be responsible for less aware forms of life on your planet. Perhaps now you realise that you are just a part of the universe and not, as some of you think, the centre of it. Show more concern!"

I now believe that the love we give to all animals, including those in our care, is as important to their spiritual evolution as it is to their wellbeing. I also understand that our interaction with them plays an equally critical role in our own wellbeing and development. "Even your little cats, Jane, they too have an important pathway to walk."

It was only while sorting through old family photographs recently that I came across a snapshot of me at the age of about three, taken in the garden of my granddad's house. My face is screwed up in a big smile and in my arms I am holding a little black kitten with white socks: yet another reminder of the power of conditioning and the sub-conscious mind.

Regular sittings with Zed continued and by October 1990 plans for a centre were becoming a reality as Tom and Jean sought a suitable property and I put my house on the market despite knowing within my heart that I did not want to leave. The outcome might have been different had I voiced my reservations, although they were known to Zed of course, who counselled caution to the group with decision-making. He was, however, also encouraging as to the possibilities of us working closely together.

"It is true that each of your minds copes differently with the problems you see, and that is no coincidence because in choosing those minds you have brought about a wholeness and completeness of understanding. Some of your minds are orientated towards scientific thought, others towards compassion and love. That does not mean that within each of you there is not love and understanding, but collectively you represent the thinking of most of this world. So you see now what we're saying; that in accepting the teaching as a passive thought and turning it into an active thought amongst all of you, the conclusions which you will develop will bear a direct relationship to the understanding of the world."

Zed also said this on the relevance of the Teachings:

"But it's more than what we say, isn't it, for if what we say doesn't strike to the very core of your being, then it's no different from any other teachings. You can read books, and much of what we say is in those books, and therefore it must be more than that to you, would you not agree? After all, we say, don't we, that the words must stand on their own, and that is true. We seek not to sensationalise them by dwelling on where they came from, we seek not to illustrate them with sensationalism: they are simple words, no different from others.

"This has to be looked at from two points of view: from the six of you and from others outside this room. Let us first look at the six of you: what makes the words special? If you look at them as purely ink on paper – nothing. But if you feel with your intuition, if you sense the motivation of love, if you are aware of the total energy within you, then they take on a special quality. In conveying the love of the universe, in understanding the unity we bring you, in realising you are just part of the whole, then the concept changes. And if you feel that love within and you know it to be true, then your awareness changes, and when your awareness changes, the intuitive wisdom within you flows.

"This happened with the Disciples of Christ: they felt one once more with the universe. This has happened with many holy men throughout your time. If this means the same to you, then when you walk from this room, the simple words will carry with them a quality of wisdom and love that no book can give you. So you may be saying the same as others, but others can see the love within you and can intuitively feel the truth of reality; then the words take on a different meaning to them. *That* is what is different between what we say and what others say. So friends, this night, examine your feelings within you, see the reality of your existence and walk with us along our pathway of love."

By November the first diagram of the Triangles of Life was given, which would eventually expand and bring together the many aspects of the Teachings into a concise and understandable form. It was immensely exciting. Here, clearly set out for all to see, was the relationship between the higher self and the mind and the different motivating factors of each. Here was the connection between all the experiences of life including suffering and the awareness of all knowledge, and here too was the way in which the higher levels of love and wisdom may come into our daily lives. I began to discover, as I still do, that by placing a problem or question against these seemingly simple diagrams, its significance within the flow of life is revealed. In a way I cannot adequately explain, the triangles had the power to draw me into their wisdom and a deeper connection within myself. The possibilities for teaching were obvious

By December I was again unwell from the pressure of work and uncertainty about the future. I was told,

"The new era is approaching and the time for you to consider some sharing of your work with those around you, for you cannot do it all. They would be happy to help but you must ask, for you have to realise too that you have physical limitations and these limitations you have chosen, and for good reason. And you will work that out yourself."

One of the things I did not understand at that stage was the shifts of energy I was experiencing and which I would continue to experience from time to time over the following years, especially after I had begun working with another medium. At that time though, I was largely unaware of the changes that were necessary to contain energy within the physical form apart from those that Malcolm had undergone during his development as a medium. How many times would I need to be told to delegate before I took notice? Ego is a sneaky thing that comes in many guises.

The 17th January 1991 was the first day of the Gulf War and the group took the decision to organise a day of public meditation for peace. The event was held in a local school hall and although attendance was not great, it was our first public expression of unity. Mo and Pat in particular were deeply affected by the outbreak of this war and were psychically aware of its effects on the civilian population. Mo spoke to Zed of how she felt very emotionally involved in current affairs, becoming upset and feeling helpless from a material point of view. With his customary kindness, Zed replied,

"You have chosen a mind with great sensitivity; if you had not, you could not do your work. But it's at times like this you must learn the lesson of true objectivity. Like the rest of us here, you see the crisis that is developing and the suffering that is being created, and as ambassadors of love, everything that happens flies in the face of what you stand for. Deeper understanding of yourself is necessary. When you are healing, we have said 'give unconditional love.' This situation is no different. The magnitude creates great emotion within you, but be objective: this is not uncaring. Be objective, otherwise how else do you avoid getting pulled in if you don't adopt that attitude?" He told the group, "You should differentiate between emotion and objectivity, as we've said before, for the depth of emotion is not a measure of your love or spirituality, but only as a consequence."

By the end of the following month there had been a ceasefire in the Gulf War and Zed had this to say,

"You ask if you were helping the world, old friends. Two sides faced each other with anger in their hearts: can you doubt now the miracle that has been achieved? For never in the history of mankind has so little loss of life happened with so much aggression. Through your thoughts you sent love to others; what possible way can this manifest itself with an aggressive situation like it was, but that one side should lose the heart to fight? There is much more heartache to come and no one will believe your influence, but we say to you, this could not have been achieved without your unity of thought. If you needed a positive demonstration of what thought can do, you have seen it with your own eyes."

Mo was asked for her feelings and answered, "I'm greatly relieved the anger has now subsided for a while but I still feel there's a lot of hatred and anger left which may take a while before it can be cleared." Zed replied, "Yes, My Eyes, but feel not hurt at such a thing, for if you give love unconditionally then you merely observe the results in an objective way. Emotion at our level plays no part. Anger and anguish, distress and hurt, are a first reaction to the way others are treating their fellow beings of experience and the planet itself."

He then gave his five points on the nature of pure love:

1. Pure love is a love untarnished by anticipation.

2. Pure love is the highest manifestation of spiritual energy.

3. Pure love embraces everything.

4. Pure love understands the emotions of the body and of the mind.

5. Pure love accepts within its arms all hatred, anger, greed and ignorance.

"You see now why it is the motivating force of the universe. You see now why awareness of its true nature is so necessary.

"We told you a long time ago of the world economic recession: give thoughts to it. The hardship it will cause will bring sadness to many and hunger to a multitude. Send thoughts, therefore, to those with political power and help to offset the imbalance that will surely come. If you look now in all corners of the world you will see it. The world sees it as isolated incidents but we see it differently, don't we Thomas? Pride, greed and ignorance. Let them know of your love. We cannot feed them, we can only give them our love, for they have choice. And their leaders tell them, 'This is the will of

God' for surely by such a statement it abrogates all responsibility from them, do you see?"

A former hotel had now been found for the spiritual centre and Jean and Tom were going ahead with the purchase although a buyer had not been found for my house. Malcolm and Pat had been promised separate accommodation there and were keen to move out of my home and into somewhere more private. It was a prospect I also welcomed. I was finally given a date for the screening of the BBC programme 'Your Life In Their Hands - A Way of Healing.'

The following passage could be said to suggest a platform for all our diverse activities:

"Whereas you may appreciate and understand the wisdom of what we say, many do not, so you have a great responsibility, all of you. And if you are truly wise then you will use your power with humility and modesty and by so doing increase the strength beyond which your minds can conceive. If you are foolish you will boast of your exploits, whether they be to heal others or to channel messages for them. You might impress them at mind level but nothing more, for as your ego increases so your power diminishes: one offsets the other in the total understanding. See our teachings now in relation to the religions of the world and see how many of their leaders fail to reach a true spiritual understanding because of what we have said. *For our word means nothing unless it carries the love of the giver*"

Basil

In my garden with Basil, 1994.

The writing on the back of this old photo reads 'Jane looks
happy but she is like this every day.'

Dr Daniel J Benor and
Barbara Ivanova.

Barbara observing
Colin Heal in dynamic
movement.

Colin Heal is spontaneously moved into this position. Note
the scars of a previous operation on his spine.

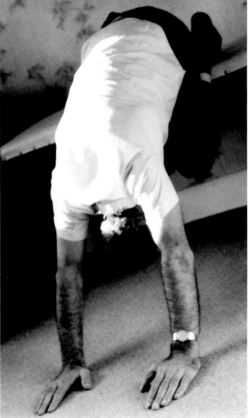

In the top photo Colin pulls his feet upwards from underneath.

The couch is used for this position which was followed by a head-over-heels.

These pictures were taken a week after Colin first came for the TV filming.

128

Chapter 9

My grandson Ben was born at the beginning of April 1991, the centre opened two weeks later and the television programme was screened a few days after that. By then Jean and Tom and Pat and Malcolm had moved into the premises and worked hard to renovate and prepare both their own accommodation and public rooms for meetings, healing and administration.

My colleagues displayed a lack of enthusiasm over the forthcoming screening of this long-awaited programme but agreed to watch it with me at my home, which they did without comment. My telephone began ringing as the last titles rolled. I was told that lines to the BBC were jammed with calls for several days following the programme from people seeking help. Requests for my telephone number were passed on to the new centre with the result that it was at full capacity from the moment it opened its doors. Requests by way of letters were forwarded to my home in bundles, many hundreds within the first couple of weeks, and their contents were heartrending in their desperation. It was a most humbling experience.

Having been warned by Stephen Rose of the possible response, I had prepared a couple of basic letter formats that I adapted for the replies. Just as Harry Edwards and his helpers had done previously, my friend Liz and I focussed absent healing with each request as it was opened and read. Mo also came to help when she could. My telephone rang continuously for weeks and despite attempts at anonymity several people arrived unannounced at the door. It was hard to manage virtually on my own, either practically or emotionally, and I felt isolated and under tremendous pressure.

There is no doubt that Stephen's film made a big impact and raised the public profile of healing in the UK and later in different countries when the BBC sold it to other networks. Although I found some of its contents a little off-course, I felt that in essence it was the first television programme to present a more balanced view of the subject. Strangely, it was to be the last programme that Stephen would produce directly for the BBC.

A room was not ready for me at the centre when it opened and so I continued to see clients at home, which was more conducive for my work anyway. However, Jean, Tom, Mo and Pat were kept fully occupied with healing appointments day after day and week after week, which although no doubt tiring for them, got the centre off to a flying start both financially and in terms of publicity. The demand for healing meant that Malcolm was the only member of the team left to answer the telephone and make the bookings, which was not a role he relished. I later learned that he assured all enquirers that the results would be the same no matter which healer they saw; information that I'm sure he believed but which unfortunately left many visitors disappointed at not experiencing the dynamic reaction they probably expected. Sad to say, the relationship between the two of us had become badly strained partly, but by no means solely, due to my inability to help with the practical upgrading of the premises due to my own workload. It now became even worse when I refused to take turns with the rest of the team with reception duties, my argument being that those who had seen the programme and travelled miles for an appointment would be justifiably annoyed to find me sitting behind a desk when they had been told I was not available. I offered to pay for someone to take my turn but this was refused. It was made increasingly clear over the following months that my presence at the centre was under sufferance.

Even more distressing to me was the realisation that those precious sessions with Zed were over. It is no exaggeration to say that I felt bereaved.

There had been no warning at our meeting with Zed on the 4th April that our time as a group was drawing to a close, although the distress within some members was acknowledged with these opening words:

"Good evening, old friends. Unload your minds and let them be at peace. Stand aside from your life this night, let the confusion within you cease. We share together a beautiful universe. And remember, through our suffering and pain we focus our minds on the reality of life and if we are wise ones, as we all are here, then we see such suffering only as a stepping stone to a better understanding."

The next meeting took place a week later and referred to the opening of the centre thus:

"We hope your centre, all of you, will develop both spiritually and philosophically to reach new heights of understanding, for this is a turning point, old friends, for you are in the vanguard of new understandings where you will look beyond the mind to the intuitive wisdom of the universe. As we warned you before, you will be against the dogma, the sectarian belief of others, the reluctance for change, and you will need broad shoulders. Seek not popularity for its own sake: seek an understanding only of spiritual reality and then everything else will follow."

On the 18th April Zed began, "Love is more important than what you write, old friend. Let go the pain in your heart. We understand. Remember, we are all one, so your turmoil is our turmoil."

These words give some indication of the distress I was in at that time and yet I still had no idea that this would be the last session together in my home. The following suggests a break in transmission, so to speak, but I had not the faintest idea that it would be some ten years or more before spoken communication between Zed and me would be resumed through another medium.

"We have a lot of new understandings to bring you but they must wait for a little while, while you adjust. You see, spiritual understanding is a little like food; you can become full and you must digest what you have eaten. Too much and you can feel ill and become sick, too little and you remain hungry. May we suggest that there is still a lot of uneaten food on your table? Thank you for letting us come."

The year that followed these events was one of the most taxing of my life. Zed had spoken of opening doors but it felt as though the power of television had flung them back so forcibly they were in danger of coming off their hinges. Coupled with the demands for healing and teaching were the strains of working in a place where I felt unwelcome. It seemed that the higher my public profile became, the more opposition I felt from Malcolm, even though most of his students and one-to-one clients came via this route. It must have been difficult for some of the others too and I sensed that Mo in particular was confused and divided in her loyalties. Both Malcolm and I were strong personalities and I came to think of our confrontations as 'King Kong meets Godzilla.'

Fortunately as it turned out, the sale of my house fell through and Jean and Tom eventually told me they could manage without my capital input, which was an enormous relief. Most of the centre's income came initially through my contacts and workshops but of course I still had the same personal overheads and mortgage that I'd had before the centre opened and my financial situation was always finely balanced. Gradually the demands created by the BBC programme lessened and the centre became a more local focus for healing and meditation classes as I moved further afield with my workshops, the first of which was in Holland.

One of the letters I received after the programme stated, 'I saw you on television. I do Reiki but I want to do what you do. Please tell me how to do this and how much it will cost.' Here we were back to the old chestnut of techniques again! The correspondent was a lovely lady named Vida who subsequently came over from Holland with her husband Max to attend a workshop and then arranged for me to present one in their home town of Zoetemeer, kindly making all the arrangements as well as accommodating me in their home with its menagerie of parrots. Fortunately, most of those attending had at least some understanding of English and my hosts were able to translate where necessary. This was the beginning of a series of opportunities to share the Teachings with diverse groups and along the way to meet more delightful and generous seekers, many of whom remain friends to this day.

Vida did not achieve the dynamic response she had hoped for but I like to think she was not disappointed. The Teachings have furnished me with insights into the nature of spiritual healing that I am more than willing to pass on but I cannot make anyone a healer, dynamic or otherwise, for that is something each individual must develop within themselves from their own innate ability. I am also deeply grateful for being given the role of teacher, for with each and every explanation of the Teachings that I share with others, and each and every question and challenge that they share with me, comes a more profound understanding for me too. What I quickly came to realise is that re-examination brings deeper perception, not because the Teachings change, but because our awareness of them changes: that is why they appear to be multi-layered. Knowledge may satisfy the mind for a while but it is of limited use unless it is absorbed and experienced. A friend once contacted me to book a weekend workshop and I had to point out that it was the same one she'd attended twice before. She was nevertheless insistent upon going ahead with the booking and told me, 'it might be the same but I learn more every time.'

I once remarked to a very self-assured person that the deeper I delve into healing the more I realise how little I know. 'Don't worry' he replied, 'I'll lend you some books.'

An important lesson to be learned is that whilst the mind considers it is in charge of our life, all the really important opportunities come through the higher self. We often call these 'amazing coincidences'. Here is a story of one of them.

Fumi Yamamoto, a young clothes designer from Tokyo, became tired of her commercial way of life and began reading and asking about the deeper issues in life such as 'what am I' and 'what is God?' This led to her attending a self-development workshop in 1991 that struck such a chord that she felt she must pursue her inner pathway, even if it meant giving up her career. She said she felt the need to be on her own and 'in Japan that is impossible' and so after much researching and pondering she booked onto a course at a small but respected School of English and left for a lengthy stay in the UK where she felt she might find some answers. One day the students were shown a video recording about spiritual healing that amazed Fumi and made her determined to meet this dynamic healer even though she had no way of knowing where she might live or how to get in touch with her. Shortly after this, Fumi and her Japanese friend were having coffee in a café when a local builder took the only available chair at their table and, to their surprise, began a conversation in Japanese. This was Barry, whose travels as a young man had taken him to Japan where he spent some time as a novice monk before learning and working as a potter for a number of years. Fumi told him about the video and the healer she wanted to meet and Barry replied, 'Oh you mean Jane Tinworth – she's a friend of mine, I'll introduce you.' And so began a long association with Fumi and her friend Miki that helped develop their healing abilities and also to take the energy of the Zed Teachings back to their homeland, for I have an image of this energy, which is the energy of love, being planted, or anchored, in different places around the world.

After about a year of operations, the centre was increasingly focussed around Malcolm's meditation and psychic development groups, although Tom and Jean continued local healing workshops incorporating the Teachings. In addition, Tom was increasingly involved with the National Federation of Spiritual Healers, later becoming a council member and trustee and, with Jean, a regional tutor. A valuable support group for healers was also held at the centre. I still had some work there but came to dread my visits when more often than not I would let myself in to a deliberately empty reception area where any messages for me were left in an 'In' tray on the desk. Where were Zed's words now? What had we really learned from these mystical teachings?

At some point Malcolm contacted me and suggested a meeting outside the centre. We sat in my car overlooking the sea while he told me that the group, excluding me of course, was to meet and take a vote on whether they wanted me to continue to be part of the work there, and he would let me know the result. We met again the following week and he said that, with great regret, they had taken the decision to proceed without me. I recall being both devastated at the rejection and at the same time greatly relieved at being free of the commitment.

Soon after this announcement I had a kind of dream, or perhaps vision would be a better description because the image is still crystal clear in my mind. This is what I recorded immediately afterwards:

'I found myself standing at the rail of a very large ocean-going ship. Malcolm was standing next to me but neither of us spoke. I climbed over the rail into a wooden lifeboat that was lowered down and down the side of the ship to the sea below. When it reached the water I took up the oars and began rowing away. My little boat cut through the water and I felt delighted by its sleek lines and the beauty of its honey-coloured varnish. From some distance away I paused and looked back at the ship with its solitary figure standing impassive at the rail, and I felt content. The hull of the ship loomed dull and black above me and I saw that from its bow a massive anchor chain held it fast to the seabed. Then as I resumed rowing away from the ship I became aware of a large bear sitting behind me in the boat, but it did not frighten me. I lay down in the bottom of the boat and the bear lay behind me and I could feel the warmth of its fur against my skin. Then I felt the sensation of its teeth sinking into my back but I felt neither pain nor fear.'

When I thought about this vision later I realised that there was a sense of total acceptance by the figure that stood beside me at the rail, as if this action were inevitable. The ship was huge but bare and I felt no sense of loss or regret as I was lowered over the side. My little boat was light and bright and clearly built for speed and I experienced a kind of joy as I rowed away. It was not until I looked back at the towering hulk of the ship that I realised it was held fast and going nowhere. The bear in my boat came almost as an addendum to the main part of the dream but it was still very important because even at the time I knew that it represented my fear. The strange thing is that I seemed to have no resistance to the bear, even when it bit me, as though it too was a necessary part of the journey I had embarked upon.

Strangely, not everyone recalled the decision-making meeting when it was discussed by some of those involved some 14 years later, and I was told the impression was that I had decided of my own free will to leave the centre. Whatever the facts were, for me the next twelve months were a time of dark depression punctuated by wonderful teaching experiences in the UK and abroad. I still believe rejection is one of the hardest emotions to deal with even though it is often the only way to break free of our attachments: a kind of stamping on the fingers to make us let go. However, the despair I felt would have been alleviated had I practised more diligently what we had been taught, as this later guidance indicated, 'In the times of loneliness when you stood upon the mountain with the winds of desolation blowing around you, if you had looked within you would have found Zed there. Always the mind looks outwards.'

Daniel Benor, who was living and working on his healing research in London at that time, suggested that I attend a conference there, the details of which I have now forgotten. What I do remember is taking a tea break and meeting an interesting young doctor from Virginia by the name of Wayne Jonas who was also keenly interested in spiritual healing. The consequence of this encounter was an invitation to an expenses-paid healing exploration meeting to be held at the Jonas's mountain retreat in the foothills of the magnificent Shenandoah Mountains. The aim of the 3-day conference was to seek common threads of understanding between differing disciplines such as Christian healing, Shamanism, North American Indian healing, Ayurveda, Qigong and psychotherapy. Wayne's invitation was directed to 'high profile healers', which as I pointed out at the time, held the risk that these practitioners might simply excel at publicity. However, it was a privilege to be invited and I gladly accepted. Each participant was asked to prepare a half-hour introduction into his or her particular practice, which in my case was billed as dynamic healing.

Composing an introduction was not difficult and yet I was not happy with what I had written: it just would not 'do', as my mother would have said. Being short of time, I decided I would re-write it on the long flight over but again, the result was not right. Wayne and his wife Susan had kindly invited me to stay with their family at their town home in Alexandria and had also arranged for me to run a workshop in Maryland before the conference, so this would give me time to have another try at the introduction. Once more I tried and failed. Eventually it came to the evening before we were due to move to the mountain retreat and I still had nothing satisfactory on paper. I went up to my bedroom to meditate and suddenly, alone there in the stillness, three simple words hit me with an impact unequal to their familiarity: they were '*God Is Love*'. Lifted clear of conditioning, I truly understood those words for the first time: this was a statement of fact: God *is* Love. It felt as if those words had been chiselled into the stone of my psyche and their meaning went beyond the mind's comprehension in their description of universal law. I knew what I had to say.

The presenters drew lots and my talk was the first. I shared my insight as well as I could along with Zed's model on love as the motivating force of life. On reflection I felt the presentation might have been too simple for some of those present but hopefully it may have resonated with others; the response was not my concern. Two days later the meeting was asked to sum up by making a list of factors common to healing and at the top of the list was the word 'love' but nobody could define what that meant and it seemed that the more they tried, the further they moved from its core. It was a very interesting exercise but I did not envy Wayne his self-imposed task of trying to draw such diverse opinions together into one research project. Within just a few years though, he had joined the respected Samueli Institute in Virginia, of which he is currently President and Chief Executive Officer. The Institute's mission, as I understand it, is to transform health care through the scientific exploration of various forms of healing.

That was my first visit to America and I was blown away by three things: the vastness of the land compared to the UK, the equally vast amounts of food that were eaten and wasted in restaurants and the huge volume of junk mail that arrived daily. Oh yes – and the number of TV channels dedicated to psychic chat shows or the raising of church funds. I felt like a real hick. This feeling was compounded when I met the other conference attendees, some of whom were indeed high profile as well as highly intelligent and successful. One very well turned out lady who billed herself as a spiritual healer opened her presentation with the declaration that she had very few 'drop-outs' because she charged for 4 sessions in advance. Her behaviour became increasingly unacceptable over the weekend until finally another lady who, like me, had tended to stay in the background and pick up other people's trash, quietly remarked to me, 'there's nothing as bad as a healer gone bad.' Wise words!

Susan Jonas also introduced me to chocolate brownies.

My father died in November 1992. He had suffered from dementia for a year but was able to see his daughter on television just before he became too ill. It had been a very hard time for my mother who, by then in her 80's, had driven herself to the nursing home to sit with him every day for many months, baking him cakes and reminding him of familiar things. It was also hard for Shirley, being the only daughter within range: just a few houses away, in fact. When the time came, it fell to her and her husband Lawrence to make the necessary funeral arrangements in addition to always being on hand for my mother in the same way they had been for both parents. Added to my great sadness when I heard the news was a concern that I was due to hold a workshop for a large number of people in Edinburgh a week or so after Daddy's death. Thankfully, Shirley and Lawrence managed to change the time of the funeral so that I could say my farewells before catching a flight from a local airport a few hours later. My parents had been married for 63 years.

My first visit to Scotland the previous year had been arranged through Nancy, whom I had met on a course in Greece: another example of the network of friends and supporters that came to be established over the years. Nancy and her then husband Ken had secured the Edinburgh College of Parapsychology for a workshop and thanks to their many contacts plus publicity from the television programme it was a case of standing room only. I have to say that I was very pleased to be working in such an esteemed establishment as the College, especially as it had been the base for the medium Helen Duncan. In one corner of the meeting room stood the white marble bust of Helen's control guide, Albert Stewart, which appeared to stare out across the assembled gathering from its empty eye sockets. That first meeting led to many wonderful contacts and further events in Scotland for years to come.

The opportunity to run a two-week course in France came through old friends of mine who had started a new life there in the Toulouse region. Foolishly, I wondered how I could find enough material to fill two weeks but I was to discover there would not be enough time for everything we needed to share. The course did not occupy the whole of each day, of course, because we had to fit in things like eating out under the trees, swimming or lying by the pool, afternoon walks in the countryside and even a daily half hour of simple domestic chores. Our delightful hosts could not have made us more welcome even though they struggled with the vegetarian menu, which they happily ignored on a group outing to the Pyrenees without me. One member of our diverse group was the artist Belinda Eaton who was living in France at that time, renovating a large mill house when she heard of the course: only she and another lady actually lived in the area. Belinda was to become a powerful psychic and healer in her own right and a kind of outreach member of a central Zed group.

The experience of being in such idyllic surroundings gave us all the time to absorb and work with the information as well as having the opportunity to discuss it at leisure and meditate together and alone. It was so relaxed compared with the crammed weekends I had been running and yet I was conscious that events like this were available only to those who could afford both the airfare and the fee, although I kept this as low as I could. However, I have to admit that I enjoyed it in spite of my concerns, not least because I too had the time and space to pursue my inner practice away from the more mundane affairs of life at home.

'Your Life in Their Hands - A Way of Healing' was now being shown on the Discovery Channel, which brought a new wave of enquiries from even further afield. One of these was from a lady called Marie in California, who had emigrated from the UK to the United States with her husband Eddie many years previously. Marie says she was determined to see me as soon as she saw the programme. She managed to find my address through her sister in England and arranged to see me whilst over on a family visit. Marie's first healing session was indeed dynamic and involved a good deal of rolling around the floor and crying but more importantly she felt strongly drawn to discovering more about healing and its spiritual roots and to sharing these with her family and friends. With this in mind, in June 1994 Marie and Ed kindly invited me into their spacious home in Palo Alto where they worked hard to publicise workshops, talks and healing sessions. For several weeks their normal life was suspended but they were more than gracious in making me welcome and comfortable. The bliss of Californian sunshine and an endless supply of fresh apricots and peaches were a special treat, as was a trip to the ocean to see the pelicans and sea otters.

One of the most memorable events of the trip came during a weekend workshop in Marie and Ed's large and elegant lounge, where the main part of the floor was covered in pale carpeting whilst the raised floor along the rear wall was of polished wood, forming an ideal dais from which to work. I discovered that, generally speaking, American groups tend to differ from their British counterparts in that they are accustomed to a more flamboyant and up-front approach to spiritual matters. Roadside billboards and television commercials promised success in love, health and wealth through a visit to this or that psychic, and magazine advertisements offered courses on instant enlightenment.

Even Church leaders had the appearance of movie stars and to be honest, I didn't even *look* like anyone special.

However, the workshop was full and seemed to be going well and we eventually came to the session of group dynamic healing, which I explained very carefully, just in case expectation might lead anyone into the realms of imagination. Participants were spaced out around the whole room, some on the carpet and a few on the upper floor, and the room became silent as the healing began. A dull thud from behind me signalled that Eddie, who really didn't believe in 'all this', had gone down and was completely stuck with his face pressed into the floorboards and unable to move despite his best efforts. Many people were standing motionless, some were gently swaying and others sitting completely relaxed. Then without warning the stillness was dramatically ripped apart as someone broke wind with the most spectacular trumpeting possible. Yet in spite of the suddenness and volume of this event, nobody moved a muscle except Marie and I who, having caught each other's eye, became red faced and doubled over as we tried to suppress our laughter. Anyone noticing my complexion and watery eyes after the session might hopefully have put them down to the normal exertion of a GDH.

Whilst in California, I met up with Daniel P Wirth whose experiments on healing medically induced skin punctures was well known and had also featured in Stephen's television programme on healing. Wayne Jonas had expressed reservations regarding the methodology of these experiments but as a layman they looked pretty impressive to me. Sadly, Wayne was right, as Dan Benor and his colleagues later proved, but of course I was unaware of this at the time of my visit. By then, Daniel Wirth and a respected researcher were running tests to measure muscle response to healing by attaching electrodes to patients during treatments and observing the results on computer screens. Their technical term for this was examining neuromuscular physiological response with a multi-site surface electromyographic (sEMG) assessment instrument. I felt these experiments were not dissimilar to the brainwave pattern work carried out years earlier by Max Cade, in which the dynamic healer Addie Raeburn participated.

Daniel Wirth invited me to take part in his experiment and I found it very interesting to watch the immediate responses of the healing on the laptop screens. In some of the tests, extreme electrical activity was recorded whilst the patients appeared to be deeply relaxed and motionless, and in others the screens monitored the long, steady brainwaves of relaxation whilst the patients were performing spontaneous and vigorous physical movements.

I also suggested that we conduct a short experiment to demonstrate that healing does not necessarily rely on the involvement of the client's mind, i.e. that a response does not depend upon suggestion or imagination. So at the beginning of the second session when there were three people patiently seated on chairs with their electrodes in place, Daniel pretended to be checking the equipment prior to my arrival at the pre-arranged time of three o'clock. However, we had secretly arranged that I would commence healing from the other end of the house at precisely 2.55 p.m., at which exact time the computer screens leapt into action, two of the clients went into dynamic movement and the third slipped into an altered state of consciousness. I was quick to explain our little deception to the puzzled subjects when I entered the room and one of them – my friend Marie - replied that she had tried to hold on for me to arrive but 'it wouldn't let me'.

A month or two later I heard that Daniel Wirth was intending to manipulate the results of the work we had done together and was asking some of the subjects to pose as if in dynamic healing so he could photograph them for an article he was writing for a yoga publication. I advised those concerned not to take part. Yet it was with a mixture of surprise and deep regret when I learned by accident a number of years later that he and another man had been imprisoned for fraudulently obtaining large sums of money from research institutions. It transpired that the experiment demonstrating that skin punctures healed faster when exposed to a hidden healer rather than for a control group that thought it was being treated by a hidden machine, was a complete fabrication. The 'volunteers' were actually employees in a café in which Wirth and his collaborator had an interest and the skin punctures had not been medically induced or assessed or, indeed, had received any healing. All this was, of course, unknown to Stephen Rose in the making of his programme, for which Daniel Wirth constructed a comprehensive replica of his sham research.

Why a qualified lawyer, as Wirth claimed he was, should choose spiritual healing for his fraudulent activities is uncertain but as Dr Daniel Benor and his colleagues stated in their Wholistic Healing Research paper on the matter, 'While the issues raised here put in question the work of a single researcher in the field of healing studies, it does not seriously lessen the robust evidence from hundreds of other studies published by respectable researchers around the world.'

Back home in England, the spiritual centre that had been born with such high aspirations suffered further conflict between its founders when Malcolm stated his need to spend more time in isolation to pursue his ambition of personal enlightenment. He was already greatly supported in this by Pat, who relieved him of dealing with telephone and other enquiries as well as absolving him from all domestic chores but his obsession left Jean and Tom with the major share of financing and maintaining a sizeable property on a very limited turnover. The situation eventually came to a head with the inevitable result that Malcolm and Pat were asked to leave, rendering them homeless yet again. On being presented with just one side of events, I agreed to them returning to my home on a temporary basis and regrettably, the centre was sold at a loss and eventually demolished and replaced by a block of apartments whilst its erstwhile owners retired to continue their healing vocation from more homely surroundings.

It is easier now to see the wisdom in Zed's words that we glossed over so lightly at the time:

'If, in the progress of what we ask, is a Centre, then a centre it must be, but have you all really considered the options? From the time this project started we have felt your insecurity and lack of direction, Jane. We don't want to dampen your enthusiasm but the function of such a place is not just to give you all a nice home but to be an educational centre. The basis should be of our Teachings, for without that there would be no purpose.'

With Susan Jonas,
Georgetown
Washington.

Workshop in Peebles, Scotland.

Dining al fresco
France 1992.

A day out with Marie and Ed Knox, San Francisco 1995.

Chapter 10.

The closure of the centre was a great disappointment and I felt especially sorry for Jean and Tom who had staked the fruits of their working life and the security of their retirement years on the project. Having Malcolm and Pat in the house again was a challenge for us all but one we initially dealt with quite well. Friends kindly made a large room available in an outbuilding of their home where I began monthly meetings on the Teachings and healing development. I also ran a few retreats further afield, some of which I shared with Malcolm before he began organising his own. He also continued to work with a small inner group of female students, one of whom was going through a divorce settlement that would later lead to providing him with a new home and work base.

Meanwhile, I decided that as I had neither the time nor financial resources to set the Zed Teachings down into book form, I could at least begin to publish them in a modest twice-yearly magazine. If I thought this would be a quick and easy option then experience would prove me very wrong!

As well as extracts from the Zed channellings, the magazine contained articles by Malcolm and me and at least one other invited contributor in each issue, plus information on forthcoming events, readers' letters and so on. Mo donated the receipts of her postal spiritual psychometry sessions towards production expenses and my task was to set out the content and basic layout using a desktop publishing programme before handing the package over to a local computer man for the technical components and finished design. We were all learning as we went along and there were many hitches before the first issue was finally collected from the printers and posted to everyone on the mailing list with an invitation to become subscribers. It was a wonderful moment.

The Zed Magazine was a slim and modest affair but quite professional in presentation. Each issue took me about two months, on and off, to put together and although the process was frequently stressful, I was pleased to at last be setting the Teachings down in print. Justification, if any were needed, came one day with a comment from a visitor who had picked up a magazine while her husband was having healing in another room. She told me, 'I've just been reading what I already knew, but didn't know I knew.' Those words sum up the Zed Teachings beautifully.

Here is a slightly edited version of one of the articles I wrote in 1995:

'This is the story of a very special teacher who gave us an unforgettable lesson on the nature of the mind. Her name is Evie and she has Down's syndrome.

After many years of living in a large hospital, Evie and a group of other women and men moved out to live together in a large house in town, the idea being to improve their quality of life and allow them the freedom of integrating with society as a whole. With the care of dedicated staff, Evie adapted well to the major change in lifestyle and began to make choices for herself and display wider aspects of her character, including a sense of humour.

All was well until Evie began to lose weight. Medical help was at best indifferent and at worst dismissive. The plump little lady, for whom food had been a delight, became thin and listless and in pain. Everyone at the home was frustrated and concerned, especially Sheila, the staff member specifically attached to Evie as friend and advocate. Evie was brought to me for healing and although she clearly enjoyed the sessions and was sensitive to the energy, her condition did not improve and so eventually, fearing that she might die, we sought spiritual guidance for her.

As the four of us – Evie and Sheila and Malcolm and I - sat together quietly in my room, Malcolm attuned to Evie and it was as if she lifted the curtain of her mind for a brief moment and allowed us to glimpse behind it. There we all shared the profound experience of what I can only call a state of bliss: the whole room was filled with the energy of love emanating from her being. No distress and no handicap existed in that place, only love, awareness and joy.

Matthew then spoke and whilst some of the guidance was confidential, some was for our general benefit. "You see before you a highly evolved soul who seeks this lifetime of experience. You see before you one who has great awareness. Seek to understand that this is her pathway. She needs love and understanding, she needs the medical help of the world about, but understand always that *this is her choice*. It is a sad reality of human existence that you do not see one before you who is enlightened, for these are special people."

The subject was continued in the next session with Zed:

'You have moved a giant step forward in your understanding of the role of the mind. You must be grateful to your friend Evie for the wisdom she passed to you all for, thanks to her, you have insight that few have experienced. You now know the nature of *your* handicap, not hers. The Ancients looked upon the mind as an impediment to development, and to a certain extent they were correct. But they did not see beyond the metaconscious to the higher self: they did not enjoy the pinnacle of clarity that you have been privileged to share, for whereas it is true that the mind is the doorkeeper to the higher self, it also protects it. Because you cannot relate to the situation you saw Evie in, because to you her door appeared firmly closed, this is not so, because she does not need to close the door on aspects of her mind which are not an active hindrance like yours.

'What you call mental handicap is used in a variety of ways to gain experience. Some originate from the law of karma which the higher self is forced to concede and others originate from the higher self for particular aspects of learning. Such experience can be gained from all levels of entity. But unlike the child who has not the awareness of the mind, the handicapped one will only concede the information that they feel willing to give, so what happened this week was not you helping Evie but Evie helping *you*. When you meditate, many of you seek to achieve an understanding and awareness which she enjoys all the time. We brought her here because, being a highly evolved soul, she would give you a greater understanding.'

Shortly after this incident, a medical diagnosis and treatment were given and Evie returned to good health, presumably because the purpose of her illness was now fulfilled by giving us her gift of understanding. We are deeply indebted to her.

Some time after this event Sheila arrived at work one day with a migraine headache. Evie met her at the door and without a word took her hand and led her up to her bedroom and sat her down. Then moving behind her, Evie placed her hands around her friend's head. After a few minutes, the pain lifted.'

I was surprised when Malcolm elected to resume regular trance sessions because he had not found the need for them since the centre opened, although I was told there had been a couple of occasions when he had gone into trance for urgent guidance to be given to the group there. These new sessions were not, however, intended to pick up where we had left off but to move Malcolm further in his quest for enlightenment. Thirteen sessions took place in my home before he left, all of which were interesting but not appropriate for me to relate here. One exception is that in the very first sitting the communicator (not Zed of course) said this: 'your task is ... to find and care for the one who is to come'. So there it was again after so many years - the message about one who is to come. I had never forgotten it and indeed, at times it had steered me towards giving credit where it was not due. Not for the first time did I wish these portents would be more explicit but at least we were now also told that the person we were seeking was female and that we would know her 'by the mark on her form'.

I continued my travels during this period, gratefully accepting invitations to teach around the UK and abroad. Zed's words were well received everywhere but I confess that I had some reservations when a contact in Dublin arranged a weekend workshop in this predominantly Roman Catholic country. I should not have worried because, as a man once said to me in California, 'Gee – these teachings take in all religions and conflict with none of them.' This certainly proved to be the case with this workshop too, where around 50 men and women (mostly women, as usual) were overwhelmingly open and enthusiastic to the point that even some of my teaching notes disappeared during the lunch break. Of course, it was a time of change in Ireland anyway, with questions being asked of the Church and clergy and so perhaps the arrival of these Teachings was just another happy coincidence.

Slowly I learned that the enthusiasm behind a few, though certainly not all, of the invitations to host events came more from the attraction to what we might now call 'celebrity' than to spiritual motivation. Occasionally I noticed disappointment when I failed to live up to someone's expectations and I also became aware that flattery would be an easy trap to fall into. However, the events themselves were always valuable as an opportunity to reach new people and Zed's guidance has helped me to understand that as long as I give my best, I am not responsible for how either my teaching or healing is received.

Malcolm's most devoted student was a gentle lady named Kim, a long-time practitioner of meditation and T'ai Chi who was in the process of making major changes in her life. Together they spent many hours searching for a place that would provide two dwellings within an environment sufficiently tranquil for their needs. Eventually such a place came onto the market; a small neglected cottage with two dilapidated wooden chalets tucked away amidst woods on the side of a hill and approachable only by four-wheel drive vehicles. Much work was required before the dwellings were habitable but in essence the place was ideal and in due course the three of them moved in – Kim, Malcolm and Pat. And Basil and I happily snuggled back into our house again.

Malcolm was more settled in his new environment. He shaved his head and dressed in the brown tunic, trousers and robe that Pat made for him; the stated object being to reflect the simplicity of his lifestyle. Some were attracted by his appearance and others chose to walk away.

Regular meetings of what was now called The Zed Foundation continued in order to discuss the magazine and any other projects. The old core group of Malcolm, Pat, Mo and me was increased by the addition of Kim and another student, Jill, and finally Jill's sister who would eventually succeed Pat as Malcolm's long-term partner. The various spheres of our activity were originally complementary but gradually the gulf between Malcolm's work and mine grew wider. Everything I did centred around the Zed Teachings and spiritual healing whilst Malcolm's work focussed on Buddhist-based philosophy. My work took me out and about with new people and places whilst Malcolm worked predominantly from home with small groups of regular students. In theory it should have been a workable arrangement.

By 1997, five editions of the Zed Magazine had been produced and although it was eagerly awaited by subscribers, its already small circulation was diminishing, partly due to a lack of publicity. At the meeting to discuss

Issue 6, it was proposed to drop the name 'Zed' from the title and replace it with 'The Foundation' to reflect the more 'open' philosophy that Malcolm and his group had now adopted: no longer was the magazine's prime role to be a vehicle for the Zed Teachings but was to reflect a variety of philosophies from a range of teachers. I felt strongly that whilst these other beliefs were already published and available, the Zed Teachings had been given into our care alone to offer to the world. I was distressed but outnumbered. It was the shape of things to come.

The situation came to a head at the end of the following year when I asked the others in the group to take over production of the magazine because I no longer had the time or energy to continue on my own. Maybe I should have said 'time or enthusiasm' but it would have made no difference because nobody volunteered and the project ended with Issue 9. It was at another meeting some months after this event that I explained that I now intended to take time out to write the Zed Teachings into book form and would therefore have to relinquish running the Foundation's administration. The inevitable result of this was that I withdrew from the group with the arrangement that I would remove my name from the Foundation's financial account but keep the Zed Teachings and all the surplus magazines. What a sad ending to this special but often troubled partnership. But in hindsight, how perfect!

All things are known in spirit, and whilst our minds struggle with anxiety, anger and regret, preparations are already in place for our next step, and the one after, and the one after that – always assuming we are awake to the opportunities, of course.

I remember listening to the national news one morning in July 1998 and being suddenly overwhelmed by a feeling of utter failure. The news was full of human conflicts and ecological disasters and the words came rushing into my mind: 'Spread the Teachings of Zed, for they are desperately needed in the world.' Would the situation be different if I had written and published the Teachings years ago? I was distraught. Sitting at my desk, I bent my head and offered a prayer from my heart. I pleaded, 'I have never asked for anything for myself before but please, if I have not failed and it is not too late, then give me a sign.'

A few days later I opened the door to Jean Wood, a lady who had come for healing following a serious injury and subsequent operation that had left her leg bent at an unnatural angle. Jean had previously responded dynamically to healing and was keen for more information so I had given her a couple of Zed magazines to read. Now she stepped into the hallway waving a magazine and said, 'I thought of you.' I didn't know what she was talking about. 'When it was on the news' she said. I still didn't understand and so she explained that the television and newspapers had reported on sightings of a huge letter 'Z' in the sky over the west coast of the UK a couple of nights previously. The event had missed me completely. I looked it up on the Internet after Jean left and this is what I found:

'LIGHT PHENOMENON SEEN BY HUNDREDS IN UK

An unusual light phenomenon, which resembled a giant letter Z, was seen on both sides of the Irish Sea after 10:30 p.m. on Friday, July 10, 1998.

According to the BBC report, "A large meteorite is being blamed for hundreds of sightings along the west coast of Britain Friday evening. Initially authorities were baffled about the source of the lights, which looked like the letter Z or the number 2."

"Throughout Friday evening, police and coastguards from Cornwall to Scotland were inundated with calls from people who spotted the light, though most came from people living around the Irish Sea."

"Coastguards in Belfast said that they had received dozens of 999 calls and admitted they had seen the light in the sky...over the north coast of Ireland. A spokesman said the light had a large Z shape."

"'It was very prominent and was due north of the (Belfast) coastguard station. We were able to watch it from the window. I can say that I've never seen anything like this before.'"

"It was a larger shape than the moon but, as we were unable to measure the distance, it was impossible to judge its actual size.'" (Editor's Note: It was a full moon Friday night.)

The Z-shaped light "appeared to be moving very slowly westwards. 'When we first saw this object, it was not completely dark (yet). It was higher than the clouds and occasionally it was obscured by passing clouds.'"

"Another report was received by Teesside Air Traffic Control near Middlesborough, who reported seeing an object resembling the letter Q in the sky west of their position."

"In a statement, the (UK) Department of Transport said, 'The sightings were as far apart as Cornwall and the Clyde (in Scotland), west of Belfast (Northern Ireland) and east to Leeds. RAF Fylingdales early warning station reported no undue activity, as did Jodrell Bank. We can only summarise it is space debris or a comet.'"

On Saturday, July 11, "an airline pilot who landed at East Midlands Airport" provided "an explanation."

"The pilot reported seeing a large meteorite entering the atmosphere as he was flying from the UK to France. He claimed to have noticed it breaking up and leaving a long trail in its wake, which was forced by winds into shapes resembling the letters." (Many thanks to John Hayes for the BBC report.)

(Editor's Comment: Excuse me, but luminous meteor trails last between five and ten seconds--twenty seconds

157

tops. They do not persist in the sky for over an hour. Whatever this phenomenon was, it was no meteor.)'

Whatever explanation anyone else might come up with, I knew without a shadow of doubt that my prayer had been answered. I also knew, as I had always known, that the Teachings that rested in my custody were of vital importance to humankind at the start of this new age, and the dramatic nature of the Z sign served to emphasise this like a huge exclamation mark. I was so very grateful to be told that it was not too late.

Relieved now of peripheral duties, I started the work of collating into readable form what was basically three years' worth of almost weekly conversations; hundreds of pages, all taken down in longhand and filling three large lever-arch files. These had already been deciphered, typed out and checked by Jean, which made the present task much easier. Still, I was anxious not to omit anything of significance as I worked backwards and forwards again and again through the transcripts, placing the various subjects into chapters and trying to build the understandings in the same careful way they had been given to us.

Zed had quite often given encouragement and guidance about setting the 'messages' into print and he once told me, 'Your own use of words is often better than ours.' This is the only point on which I disagree with my friend in spirit, for I have come to understand that the words themselves carry the energy of the giver and so when I repeat Zed's words, they connect with the stream of love and wisdom with which he conveyed them. Several psychics have independently told me that they can see this happening in my energy when I teach. Above all though, I believe there is a very real danger in changing words that has affected many holy teachings: the danger is that of *interpretation* and it is a trap I have come across many times. For example, I may find that the grammar in a particular passage from the transcripts is not wholly correct or perhaps the meaning is not instantly obvious and consequently the temptation is to change a word or two to suit my perception of how it should read. But of course my perception is limited to the level of my awareness coupled with my conditioned mind and so the altered passage could then express my personal opinion rather than the truth, however well intentioned I might be.

As I see it, my task is to pass on these Teachings in as pure a form as I can, and after that it is up to the listener or reader to make of them what they will. As I tried to make very clear in the introduction to 'The Bridge of Awareness', no dogma is attached to the words, as Zed explains:

"The teachings must be examined and choices made. Don't expect others to come to the same conclusions that you have immediately. Each person will interpret an abstract painting differently from the artist, but the important thing is that it starts them thinking."

Compiling the messages into book form was a detailed but wonderful task that kept me happily occupied for months. The draft was almost complete and at long last these dimensional teachings were nearing the stage when they could be parcelled up and sent to a publisher – or so I thought. The reality was that as I wrote the last line of the last chapter, I knew the book was not finished and that, for the time being, there was nothing more I could do. I had no idea why or what more was needed: I just knew I could go no further and so with great reluctance I laid it aside. As I have said before, the really important events of our lives are not orchestrated by the mind and I was certain that when the time was right I would again take up the metaphorical pen and do whatever was required, which eventually proved to be the case.

By way of contrast, a few years after Malcolm and I had gone our separate ways, I came across one of his brochures that began: 'Once a Buddhist Monk, now a Zen Master...' This struck me as a strange statement because in all the time I worked with him his only contact with official Buddhism was when he met a British-born senior Buddhist monk who happened to be staying at a house we had booked for a retreat. However, it appeared that he and his new partner had set up a school of Buddhist philosophy that, as far as I understand from its published literature, promotes an agnostic view of life where religion and faith are merely tools of survival created by the brain to counteract its fear of death. Furthermore, it promulgates the idea that there is no proof of an afterlife. I would not presume to question Malcolm's chosen path but I can't help wondering where he now places those experiences we shared that seemed so real to him at the time: the voice that first spoke to him in the wood, his experiences with Matthew, his role as a medium, his glimpses into past lives and awareness of spirit entities: were these too just fantasies conjured by the brain? Personally, I would rather face the challenges of faith then sit on the fence of agnosticism.

There is a wonderful book written in the 1940's by the architect Laurence Temple, recording channelled messages from St Francis of Assisi to 'his brother Lorenzo' (Laurence). Written in a most beautiful and evocative form of English, the communications speak of 'families' or groups of souls that experience with and for one another in successive lifetimes: something I have become more acquainted with over the years. But the book, The Shining Brother, also demonstrated to me how the same communicator could make himself known through a number of different channels, in this case with one medium even picking up in mid-conversation where another, many miles away, had left off. It was confirmation of what I already knew by then: that my partnership with Zed was not over. Indeed, it never could be.

Chapter 11

I am sometimes asked what is the most dramatic or amazing reaction to dynamic healing I have witnessed. The ones with Bill Hoskins and Spencer recorded in this book are certainly very high on the list but there have been many others and they have all enriched my life. Both my sons are open to the effects of dynamic healing and Stuart especially is amongst its more spectacular exponents in terms of spontaneous movement. On one memorable occasion when Stuart and his wife and their son were relaxing in my living-room, I began to give him healing on some minor sports-related injury, whereupon his body assumed a powerful control of its own, propelling him around the room in a variety of rigorous exercises whilst we tried to get out of the way. This performance continued for some time and caused much amusement in the 3 observers, which in turn began to irritate Stuart. However, try as he might, he could not stop it and in desperation he finally declared, 'I've had enough of this - I'm going home!' and made a move towards the door, whereupon he appeared to be lifted off his feet and thrown sideways over the end of the sofa. By this time we were almost helpless with laughter. Eventually he was released sufficiently to regain some control and leave, although I was later told that the spontaneous movements continued on and off at home throughout that evening.

Of all these spectacular displays though, I think the most amazing response to my healing happened when I was called to see someone with chronic fatigue syndrome – myalgic encephalomyelitis (M.E.). Before his illness the man had been a professional sportsman. Now he was mainly confined to his bed and reliant upon carers to attend to even his most basic needs. Over the several years of his illness his family had called in specialists and taken him around the country for treatment from a variety of alternative practitioners, all without success. No doubt I was just another straw to clutch at. He was very weak on the day I called and he lay silent and relaxed with closed eyes as I sat by the bed and began the healing. After a while, I can't recall how long, I looked at him and saw something extraordinary: every part of his body, including his facial muscles, was completely motionless except for his scalp, which was gently moving from side to side across the top of his head.

After the session the man remarked that he had found it a most sensuous experience but made no mention of feeling anything else. Whether or not it had any long-term effect on his condition, I have no idea because I learned long ago to simply offer the healing and leave it at that. Attempts to evaluate are a waste of time and carry the dangers of expectation and ego.

There was a fashion in healing circles at one time that stated that anyone can be a healer, presumably founded on the premise that the love of God is within everyone and therefore just needs to be brought out. This thinking is understandable and I have no doubt that the capacity for love and compassion is indeed inherent within the essence of every human being and that thoughts of this nature are a vital and potent influence in the world. In that respect we are indeed all healers. However, whether an individual is energetically suited to be the kind of healer able to channel a particular kind of energy and whether this is their chosen pathway this time round is a quite different matter. This is why courses that offer to make someone into a healer need to be treated with scepticism, for no amount of knowledge or techniques will produce a healer unless that person already has a spiritually developed healing ability within them, whether they know it or not. In other words, healers are born and not made. This is not say of course that healing courses are wrong - how could I say that when I have presented so many myself - it simply means their prime objective must be to assist individual development and this has to include the inward path of meditation and self awareness. If this pathway is pursued then the person will intuitively know how to practise, for the act of spiritual healing is not something we do, but an expression of what we are. For this reason I sometimes feel dismayed at the dumbing-down of spiritual healing by organisations in their enthusiasm to recruit fee-paying students.

As our friend Doctor John realised, spiritual healing may be triggered by the mind but its essence and power lie way beyond it, for the energy of spiritual healing is the very life-force itself, the motivating force of the universe that seeks to align everything with its own perfection. Thought, therefore, is the mechanism that connects the subject to the force.

So how do we know if we have that healing ability within us and if it is to be expressed in this lifetime? I think the answer must be that the awareness of our pathway will make itself known to us, just as gifted musicians, writers or mathematicians, for example, will be pulled inexorably in a particular direction. For some healers, that inner knowing can be there from childhood whilst for others it may emerge at any time later as a consequence of their own illness, or compassion for the suffering of someone else, or by being drawn to a spiritual activity or setting. It may even emerge through a mystical experience. However it happens though, it could be said that this gift is too important *not* to make itself known. But again, as Zed points out, always there is choice.

Just as this precious gift will emerge if it's meant to, no amount of wishing will make it happen if it's not there. A man once contacted me because a local psychic had told him he had 'healing energy'. He subsequently attended various healing workshops and read copiously on the subject but for some reason decided that he wanted to be a dynamic healer and offered to pay me any fee I asked if I would teach him how to do it. No amount of explaining why this was not possible would dissuade him, and his attitude implied that I was deliberately withholding information to keep him from his goal. He was certain that the psychic's prediction was correct but flatly refused to meditate as she suggested because he 'just couldn't bear to sit still'.

The man also came to me for healing on a chronic health condition for many months but gained little benefit because he insisted upon talking his way through every session until eventually I became so exasperated that I refused to give him another appointment on the basis that it was a waste of my time and his money. After a lengthy interval he rang again and pleaded for help and this time I agreed to see him on condition he didn't speak a word. The resulting session was very interesting in that he actually kept silent during the healing and afterwards reported that for the first time ever he had experienced something – terrible pain! He said that during the 40 minutes or so of lying on the couch he had felt every pain he'd ever had, in every part of his body. I have no idea why, although I might have my suspicions. As far as I am aware, the conviction that he was a healer remained with him to his dying day but sadly, and with equal conviction, I am sure he was not and that the desire that drove him came solely from his mind. There is no doubt that he desperately wanted to be healer, but why? Was he driven by an inner compassion to be of service to others or perhaps by a different image of what is it to be a healer?

This question might also be applied to another man who wrote to me some years later from Romania with a request for lessons on the dynamic healing he had seen or read about. Once again I did my best to explain that dynamic healing is not a technique but a spontaneous response to a certain frequency of spiritual healing and cannot therefore be learned. Perhaps there was a language problem but the man, who explained that he was already a Reiki Master and practitioner of a number of other therapies, refused to take 'no' for an answer. He then insisted that he wanted to know how to raise his awareness to achieve these results and so I sent him a copy of the recently printed 'Bridge of Awareness', thinking that would be the last I would hear of him. However, a month or two later I received an email telling me that I could now see his dynamic healing on a video he had posted on the internet. The spectacle of this man waving his arms at a small group of people like a magician performing tricks whilst they obliged by putting themselves into various postures made me feel angry, then insulted and finally exasperated. Even before tuning in to the energy I could see this was no display of true healing, dynamic or otherwise, and whilst I was tempted to post a comment to that effect I decided that such deceit would be likely to reap its own rewards without my intervention.

There is no getting away from the fact that a few charlatans exist, like a certain man in the UK who purports to perform psychic operations by drawing invisible tumours from stomachs and throwing them in a bin. The really sad thing is that hundreds of individuals still file through his room for a quick 'treatment' despite his exposure on television as an obvious fraud. This may speak of gullibility or desperation on their part but there is no doubt in my mind that anyone who uses the pretence of being a healer to knowingly exploit the sick and disabled for their own gratification and financial gain is hardly better than the priest that abuses children. Practising the Five Points of Pure Love in relation to such people is sometimes a struggle.

I count myself very fortunate that the realisation of my own healing pathway came in such a profound and physically transformational manner that choice was virtually irrelevant because left largely to my own devices I was able to pursue this new direction without opposition. This is not the case for many emerging healers and psychics for the world is full of sceptics, even within our immediate circle, some of whom may be genuinely anxious when their loved one becomes embroiled in something they consider weird or alien to their religious beliefs. Such challenges are important though, because they force the individual to examine their own beliefs and commitment. No-one said it would be easy!

The choice that Zed speaks of obviously determines the direction we take in any aspect of our lives, including our spiritual pathway. Healers, mediums and spiritual teachers especially have to be constantly on their guard against the danger of confusing what might be called the personality thoughts that arise from the conditioned mind, with intuitive thoughts that are informed from the higher self. My own experience and observations have confirmed what many teachings of the past have stated: that even those with advanced spiritual awareness may be led astray by the ego, which may be defined as the personality's image of, and desires for, itself. The point is beautifully illustrated by The Mirror of Illusion story in The Bridge of Awareness. Only meditation and vigilance can teach us the origin of our thoughts. Only by constantly recognising and dealing with unhelpful thoughts can we hope to achieve a pure mind.

We all need to understand that spiritual awareness comes hand in hand with an equal measure of inescapable karmic accountability and therefore the greater the awareness, the greater the accountability for our thoughts and actions in this life and those that follow. Karma is not, as some would have it, a 'bad' thing: karma is simply a Universal Law that ensures our progress from ignorance to ultimate awareness through lifetimes of experience. In other words, what we don't understand this time round, we'll have the opportunity to grasp in another. And with the growth in awareness comes an increasingly powerful reservoir of energy at our disposal and although there may be a reluctance to use the word 'power' for the spiritual force within us, that is actually what it is. Those that really understand will use this sacred energy carefully and compassionately in the service of others, whilst those that choose to use it for self will inevitably incur karmic justice of a less agreeable kind.

As I have tried to explain, the phenomenon of spontaneous, self-correcting movements in spiritual healing were outside my previous knowledge and arrived unexpectedly and to my complete amazement. The reason I chose the label 'dynamic' was because that is how it appeared to be – a force that is alive and in movement *of itself.* I have never considered that I *make* these movements happen but rather that they simply happen in my presence. It is therefore sensible to accept that some part of me beyond my mind is a motivating factor in this kind of healing process and I have of course sought an understanding of what that might be.

A study of the Teachings of Zed (and I mean 'study' rather than 'reading') shows the origin and pathway of the healing force from source to recipient plus the degree to which it is available to all healers and the obstacles that may hinder its progress. This is equally true for dynamic healing which is an aspect of spiritual healing. When I asked Zed about it in the early days he replied that every force has a wavelength and the healing force is no different. Whilst I struggle to get my head around this kind of thing, I took this statement to mean that the healing force has its own 'identity', a concept that has interesting implications. Zed also explained the emergence of dynamic healing in my work by saying that whereas the way in which the power manifests was previously a small reflex, 'it is now greater and really undulates', and so 'dynamic healing is the density of a type of power'. He also said that some people respond in a certain way to dynamic healing, 'which oscillates at a certain frequency'.

In simple terms, all healing is the interaction between three elements: the spiritual healing force, the healer and the recipient. Just as the degree of healing energy may differ from healer to healer, so the way it is received will also differ according to certain factors and it is always important to be aware that healing is a spiritual process orchestrated on a spiritual level. However, it is also necessary to accept that little can take place unless the receiver's mind is open and willing, as illustrated in the account of the man who talked through every session. The higher self of the recipient knows both the spiritual reason for their suffering and what is needed to alleviate it, neither of which is known to the healer's mind. It therefore follows that specific expectations as to an outcome are of more hindrance than help and this is one of the hardest lessons for any healer to learn. The two words that sum this up for me are *surrender* and *trust*. Both are extremely challenging.

When I began my healing journey over 40 years ago, I could see no further than the person's pain and my desire to take it away. This wasn't exactly wrong but it had the downside of leaving me with a sense of failure if the condition didn't respond as I thought it should. It took a long time for me to learn that however well-intentioned I may have been, I was trying to impose my *will* on someone's spiritual journey instead of surrendering it to the greater force. The temptation to intervene is particularly strong when a healer is asked for help when someone is critically ill or in the process of dying and their loved ones are in a state of high emotion. Although I have been guilty of this myself, the best example I can give is from the book The Shining Brother that I mentioned before.

Laurence Temple was asked by a friend to give healing to a desperately sick relative. This is what he wrote: 'When I saw the young boy lying silent and barely conscious my heart went out to him. As I placed my hand on his head he smiled, and I prayed with all the force of my will for his recovery.' On the third day Temple received a note from a spiritual medium friend who asked, 'What are you attempting? Come and see me.' When he arrived his friend said, 'Are you attempting to heal someone?' He said he was and she asked, 'Is it God's will that he should be healed or is it just yours?' With great honesty Temple admitted that the question brought his thoughts to a very sudden focus and he told her, 'I am ashamed to say that I am endeavouring to impose my will' to which she replied, 'Are you aware that if you succeed you will be incurring responsibilities that you cannot very well meet?' He said he didn't realise that and he was told, 'Brother, you must never intrude. ... You are holding this boy back.' The medium then counselled him to 'Stand by the boy and release him in your mind. Say 'God's will be done' and he will then be free to go. Tonight as you sleep, you will help him cross the difficult country. That is what you were wanted to do: you mistook your work.' Laurence Temple did as she suggested and the young man died that night.

I have to admit that there have been occasions when I have actually been tempted to ask for someone's death to be hastened, either because they were suffering awful pain or because they appeared unconscious and were dying slowly, but this too would have been imposing my will on another, which is a subjective emotional reaction and not, as many imagine, true compassion. In my view, compassion is indeed a response to suffering but an objective response from a higher level that overrides the conditioned judgement of the mind. In other words, not the head but the heart. Training the mind not to jump in and impose its judgements and desires in a healing situation is undoubtedly hard but something every healer needs to be aware of. Unfortunately, the distinction between emotional reaction and compassion is little understood, even within many spiritual settings.

I have no doubt that each one of us comes into a lifetime with a blueprint of things to experience and when those things are accomplished we are free to return Home. It may even be possible that a person's illness and death are the most important reasons for them incarnating this time. The problem is that our earthly minds cannot see the bigger picture and so we are quite naturally locked into our grief, even when our inner knowing tells us that we step from one phase of life to another. I can only imagine that the trauma of loss must be even more terrible and lasting for those who believe that death is absolute and nothing but annihilation awaits us at the end of physical life. Indeed, holding such views must surely affect the way a person lives their life. In

1693 William Penn, a founder of the Quaker Movement, wrote about life and death in his beautiful 'Fruits of Solitude' which includes the line, 'We cannot love to live if we cannot bear to die.'

Another priceless quotation came from my younger grandson, Christian, when he was about 8 years old. He had obviously been mulling something over in his head when he came to me and said, 'Can I ask you something, Narnie?' 'Of course.' I replied. 'Well', he said earnestly, 'what's the point of being alive if you're just going to *die*?' I was enormously impressed. Here was a child seriously considering the question every person should ask: the reason for their existence. Needless to say, Christian's searching opened the way for a discussion on the soul and reincarnation which in some countries of the world are an accepted part of everyday belief.

I am indebted to the kind of experiences I have shared with Spencer and other terminally ill clients who have not only trusted me in life but informed and comforted me after their death. Another of these was a long-time acquaintance whose reaction to reaching the final stage of his illness was to be very angry and obviously disinclined to receive more healing as he sat cocooned and frail in a darkened room. With some reluctance on my part as well as his, I sat with him and was intuitively guided to speak to him very carefully about the transition he would make and particularly the joy he would experience at the reunion with someone who had been very dear to him, to which he appeared fairly non-committal. He died a week or two later and I decided not to go to his funeral, which I knew would be very well attended because he had been a popular man in his community. I was sitting with a medium friend on the morning of the service when she said, 'I have to tell you there is someone here with a message for you. It's Mike and he's saying to tell Jane 'Thanks for the healing – it worked a treat!' She went on to say that Mike was very excited but in a hurry and said he 'had to go now'. I looked at my watch and saw it was a couple of minutes after the start of his funeral. He had always been late for appointments!

Mike's message that the healing worked a treat was important not just for me but for all healers because it confirms that what we do goes way beyond alleviating or curing illness and disability. At the time of death spiritual healing acts a kind of bridge by creating an energy within which the slower vibrations of the physical frame can be loosened and raised, thereby allowing easier movement into the finer dimensions of *being*. I understand that this process takes a varying length of earth-time to complete depending upon the physical state of the body and both the mind-awareness and spiritual-awareness of the individual. Obviously the more spiritually aware and less materialistic a person is, the more prepared they are for the transition and consequently the smoother it will be. I used to be sceptical of accounts by members of the Spiritualist Movement about 'spirit hospitals' with 'spirit doctors and guides' tending to newly-deceased (or newly returned) patients but I now admit that my scepticism has waned in the light of experience and I believe that we are indeed healed back into spirit life when necessary. Of course, whether there are replica hospitals or not is a matter of speculation.

The benefit of healing someone from physical life back into non-physical life begs this question: would it be equally beneficial to heal a baby from non-physical life into physical life? Or perhaps this simply emphasises the importance of welcoming every conception and birth with love.

Of all the big life issues, the subjects of death and suffering are the most difficult for our minds to comprehend. The Asian tsunami of 26th December 2006 was a trauma of epic proportions that caused terrible suffering and loss of life. Shortly afterwards, a television programme approached leaders from a range of religions and philosophies with the age-old question that I posed in chapter 1 of this book; 'If there is an all-powerful God of Love, why did He allow this to happen?' I was fascinated to see that most of the religious leaders 'fudged it' and not one was able to give a definitive answer. Perhaps the most direct response came from the Buddhist who stated that 'suffering is universal', which essentially took God out of the equation.

From the spiritual healer's point of view the question is essential, for if suffering is simply something bad that exists *outside* of the Divine Intelligence (however we perceive that to be) then it needs to be zapped – eliminated – made to disappear. However, if suffering is *within* the divine plan then our relationship with it drastically alters.

If Zed had been included in that television interview after the tsunami he would probably have responded that God is a God of Unconditional Love and not the god of judgement that religion has turned Him into. God therefore does not select who should suffer and who should not, for such things are within the universal laws of karma and reincarnation and therefore important tools for raising awareness. More than anything, these universal laws give mankind *choice* and therefore *self-responsibility* for his thoughts and actions which in turn interact with *all* life, including the planet itself. So the Buddhists are right in saying that suffering is universal, but to blame it on a vengeful God or inventing an opposing demonic force isn't the answer either. Universal laws exist in the same way that a law of gravity keeps our feet planted on the planet, and all laws are encompassed within the One.

Harry Edwards saw illness as bad and even wrote of the 'evil of cancer' as if it had some malign intent of its own. But cancer, as with all illness, is a consequence and a tool and not some random visitation. Hard though it undoubtedly is to accept, I am certain there is a purpose in all suffering. Working with our suffering in order to find that purpose is the very reason for its existence, for what else would drive us to look in a different direction? Would we strive to discover a meaning to life if it was a bed of roses from beginning to end?

I once had a personal demonstration of trying to work with a problem when I returned from a teaching trip to America with severe back pain. This was probably the physical result of a massage from an enthusiastic masseuse that displaced a small bone in my foot, combined with dragging a heavy suitcase through airports. Being exhausted from the long-haul flight anyway, I took to my bed convinced that a good rest would put it right. It didn't. For the next couple of days I tried to give myself healing and work with the pain, searching my mind for a deeper meaning, but to no avail. I rang Mo and begged her to give me healing and of course she came hurrying over but surprisingly this didn't do the trick either. With some difficulty I then took myself off to the chiropractor where the problem with my foot was diagnosed but my back was too inflamed for anything more than gentle massage and I therefore hobbled back to my bed. I had now been laid up for more than a week and I didn't like it. Then one day I felt the need to get myself into my healing room and meditate regardless of the pain. I sat in my chair and tried to relax and all I can recall of that session is that at one point I saw an image of myself as a little girl and that was all – no accompanying setting for her, no experience she was going through – just a fleeting image like looking at an old photograph. But strange though it may seem, at the end of the meditation I stood up and walked from the room without pain. It seems to me at this distance in time that something in my past needed to be touched and set free, even though it wasn't necessary for it to lodge in my conscious mind.

Perhaps the question we need ask ourselves is not why we suffer but why we don't heal.

My work as a spiritual healer continued for some time after I had completed the draft of The Bridge of Awareness but the teaching side gradually lessened, allowing me to spend more time writing and enjoying my family and friends and my home and garden. The planet healing group continued to meet regularly, aware of the dire state of the living Earth in a way it wasn't when the first warnings were received in 1988. The concept of retirement from my spiritual work was, and is, totally foreign to me because I feel it is the very core of my being. However, any thoughts I may have harboured about doing the same things but at a more leisurely pace were soon dispelled as I was presented with a new and ultimately wondrous extension of my pathway; one that would build on The Teachings of Zed and yet have its own parallel direction. But the telling of this must wait until it has come to fruition.

In the meantime I see that my journey has been carefully planned from a point long before my entry into this lifetime to the unknown time when I shall step from this physical frame, and beyond that. Like everyone else, I came with certain tasks to complete, the opportunities to fulfil those tasks and the choice to accept or not. No doubt I have made many wrong choices and perhaps choices that seemed wrong but weren't. It's hard to see the whole picture from the confines of the mind. What I am absolutely certain of is how blessed I have been, and still am - including all the trials of life. Especially the trials.

BIBLIOGRAPHY

The Aquarian Gospel of Jesus the Christ: Levi Dowling

Spiritual Healing: Scientific Validation of a Healing Revolution. Daniel J Benor. www.wholistichealing research.com

Wholistic Healing Research paper re Daniel P Wirth: Jerry Solfvin, Eric Leskowitz and Daniel J Benor.

Ron Staley. Wholistic Healing Publications vol.5 no.2. May 2005.

The Awakened Mind: Biofeedback and the development of Higher States of Awareness. Maxwell Cade & Nona Coxhead. Element Books.

Alec Harris: The full story of his remarkable physical mediumship. Louie Harris. (revised edition) Saturday Night Press Publications 2009.

You Don't Know John Cain? Pat Sykes. Van Duren 1979.

The Shining Brother. Laurence Temple and Greta Freund.

Silver Birch Books. Spiritual Truth Press www.silverbirchpublishing.co.uk

The Two Worlds of Helen Duncan. Gina Brealey & Kay Hunter. (reprint) Saturday Night Press 2008.

A Guide To The Understanding & Practice Of Spiritual Healing: Harry Edwards (and other books). www.sanctuary-burrowslea.org.uk

George Chapman, Healing Hands: J. Bernard Hutton. www.michael-chapman.co.uk

FOOTNOTE

This book covers the main events in my life up to roughly the turn of the century. The years from then to the time of writing have been as full of spiritual twists and turns as those that preceded them; frequently amazing, sometimes painful, never dull. The new chapter that opened when the old one closed is not yet complete. I know I shall be guided to set it down on paper when the time is right and in the meantime there is still much to work on with the Teachings of Zed.

The task of gathering together to send healing to our planet must continue and grow if life here is to survive. The interconnectedness of everything is encapsulated in this statement from Zed: 'Be aware that what you do to the planet today, the planet will do to you tomorrow.' It is time to accept responsibility.

Although my ageing frame copes pretty well with the everyday business of life at the moment it can no longer retain the strength of healing energy in the way it once could and I have therefore stepped back from my work with individuals. This is not important because the dynamic healing aspect has served its prime objective of paving the way for the Teachings and there are many other aware healers willing and waiting to help those in need. Links to finding a healer can be found on the World Awareness Trust website.

It has not been appropriate to mention the many hundreds of wonderful people who have come for healing or attended and hosted talks and workshops and supported my work in many ways. But I thank you all for sharing this part of my journey and for allowing me to be a part of yours.

JT

2012

World Awareness Trust

www.worldawarenesstrust.org